10 Writing Prompts That Work (and the stories to prove it)

C. Dennis Moore

Published by Shrine Keepers Publishing, 2016.

10 WRITING PROMPTS THAT WORK (AND THE STORIES TO PROVE IT)

First edition. September 14, 2016.

Copyright © 2016 C. Dennis Moore.

ISBN: 979-8231480944

Written by C. Dennis Moore.

Also by C. Dennis Moore

an Angel Hill short
Carlotta Valdez
Flagpole Sitta
Woolly Muffler
Private Helicopter
Problems and Bigger Ones
Jack the Lion
Old Hat
Terminal Annex
Wrecking Ball

Holiday Horrors
New Year's Day
Martin Luther King, Jr. Day
Groundhog Day
Ash Wednesday
Valentine's Day
Presidents' Day
Saint Patrick's Day

LATE-NIGHT DOUBLE FEATURES
Playground of the Gods
House of Limbs
Coming Down the Mountain
Revenge of the Roach King
Maggie Andrews Gets the Facts
Son of Man
The Legend of Mr. Cairo

Mini Collections
Five Fates
Five Fantasies
Five Furies

standalone shorts
Blood Bitch
Plaything
Illusion is a Synonym for Dream
Raw Materials
The Caterpillar
In the Town of Broken Dreams
Working for the Fat Man
The League of Liars
Biscuithead
The Fish in the Fields
The Envy of Falling Leaves
Road to Nowhere
The Timesmiths

The Angel Hill novels
The Man in the Window
The Ghosts of Mertland
The Flip
Housequake
The Third Floor 2: Suicide House
The Third Floor

The Monsters of Green Lake
The Werewolves of Green Lake
The Vampires of Green Lake
The Witches of Green Lake
The Demons of Green Lake

Writers' Library
10 Writing Prompts That Work (and the stories to prove it)
Doing it Write
Writing Rules
Shut Up and Write

Standalone
Aftermath
Terrible Thrills
Bloodletting
Dancing on a Razorblade
The Dichotomy of Monsters

Love Jones

What the Blind Man Saw

Camdigan

Kung Fu Sasquatch

Science Fiction Double Feature (Foodies of Mars variant)

Science Fiction Double Feature (Purple Haze variant)

So Quake With Fear, You Tiny Fools!

The Nightmare Corridor

Inside

The Only Way Out is Through

The Organ Grinder

Revelations

Alter

The Lonely Man: Road to The Third Floor 2

Red House

Fluke

The American Way Vs. Dr. Brain

Welcome to the Trust

Table of Contents

There are a lot of writing prompt books out there. From what I've seen, they offer prompts to get you writing, but not necessarily to get you writing a *story*. I have a book, 642 THINGS TO WRITE ABOUT, and while it's a great exercise book with things like "What your desk thinks about at night" and "Five things that always get you in trouble", neither of these are really going to prompt a publishable story or novel. This book, however, will do just that, backed up by examples of the stories I wrote from said prompts, just for a little extra inspiration.

NOTE: While most of these stories are geared toward horror, because that's what I write, the prompts will work for any genre or length.

A lot of writers listen to music as they write, and for the struggling author who wants to get something down on paper, but has no ideas, music can be an excellent prompt. **As you sit at your computer, music blasting, take the title of the song you're listening to RIGHT NOW and use that as the title of a story.** Another excellent way to spark an idea is to list a lyric from the song and use that as the title, a first line, or a plot point.

I've written many stories in this way including:

1. Blood Bitch (from the song of the same name by Cocteau Twins)
2. The Legend of Mr. Cairo (inspired by "The Friends of Mr. Cairo" by Jon and Vangellis)
3. Camdigan (inspired by a line in "You've Been Around" by David Bowie)
4. Goodbye (the title of a Prince song)
5. Coming Down the Mountain (inspired by a line in "Comin' Down" by the Meat Puppets)
6. Astrid Like a Candle (inspired by the song "Melt" by Siousxie and the Banshees)
7. Senses/Mr. Grin, the Glistener (two stories inspired by a line in "Bad Apples" by Guns N' Roses)
8. If I Was Your Girlfriend (inspired by the Prince song of the same name)
9. Billy Ray's a Good Boy (inspired by the song "Son of a Preacher Man" by Dusty Springfield)
10. Terrible Thrills (inspired by a line in the song "Science Fiction/Double Feature" from the ROCKY HORROR PICTURE SHOW soundtrack)
11. Working for the Fat Man (inspired by the Escape Club song

of the same name)

12. In the Town of Broken Dreams (inspired by a line in the Ricky Nelson song "Lonesome Town")

13. The Garden (inspired by the Guns N' Roses song of the same name)

14. Monday (inspired by a line in the Escape Club song "Working for the Fat Man")

15. Satanic Mechanic (inspired by a line in the song "Sweet Transvestite" from the ROCKY HORROR PICTURE SHOW soundtrack)

16. Baby Pink Lipstick (inspired by a line in the song "What Ever Happened to Saturday Night?" or "Hot Patootie—Bless My Soul" depending on which version you have, also from the ROCKY HORROR PICTURE SHOW soundtrack)

17. Broken Man (inspired by a line in "(Segue)—Algeria Touchshriek" by David Bowie)

18. My novel HOUSEQUAKE (taken from the title of the Prince song of the same name)

And finally the story included in this book. See if you can guess what song inspired this title:

PURPLE HAZE

· · · ·

HE BROKE THE SURFACE, gasped in a lungful of air, and whipped his head around, flinging water from it in great crystalline drops. When his vision cleared he peered through water-logged lids to see where he was. The sun shone down, blinding in its brilliance and heating everything to near-oven temperatures. He scanned his location and appeared to be waist-deep in a small lake, only a few yards from shore.

He trudged through the water, which felt very thick, thicker than water should, he thought, toward the shore. Once out, he collapsed, still gasping, holding his head, which was pounding. He tried to get his bearings. He sat up and looked around again and had no idea where he was.

Judging by the starkness of the landscape, the bare, dry hills in the distance, it looked like he was in the desert. But how did he get here? And on the heels of that question was another: if not here, where should he be?

He couldn't remember. Becoming suddenly very aware of his own body, he looked down at his hands, at his clothes, then felt his face, and realized he couldn't remember his own name. He had a vague recollection of what he looked like, but everything else that went with that was a blur.

The sun was unforgiving. He saw nothing in any direction, only rocks and this lake—in the middle of nowhere.

What is going on? he wondered.

A short breeze was his only reply.

He needed to take action. He chose the hills because they were the only thing in sight that broke up the endless nothing of the desert. While all else was static, those hills offered some kind of promise.

He took off in that direction, unsteady on his feet. His stomach rumbled and he wondered when the last time was that he'd eaten anything. He considered drinking from the lake to at least put something in his belly, but then he remembered how sluggish he'd been climbing out of it and couldn't bear the thought of putting any of that stuff inside him.

He'd have to make do until he was rescued, or found some way to rescue himself. Meanwhile, he took the opportunity of his long walk to those hills to plunge the depths of his memory and try to figure out what was going on.

His clothing appeared to be some kind of uniform, but he didn't see any patches or insignia. There was a name stenciled onto it over his right breast, but the faded letters were barely readable. It looked like something that started with a K.

Keith? Kevin? Kenny? Kyle? None of these sparked any memories.

He tried to determine the last thing he remembered, but even that proved impossible. It wasn't just the recollection of detail, but the very process of forming coherent thoughts. He could see the images in his mind, he had the general shape of an idea he wanted to develop, but the words for it, the execution . . . his mind was a total blank. All he could do was focus on the walk ahead of him. He got the hills in his sights, then put his head down against the glare of the sun, and moved.

Every few minutes he looked up to make sure he was still on track and every time he found himself veering off in one direction or another. His sense of balance felt off.

He kept his ears tuned to the sounds of the desert, trying to stay alert in case a rescue vehicle was anywhere nearby. His eyes scanned the area for any signs of life. But even after what was surely nearly an hour of walking, and the only thing he saw were a few scattered and empty water bottles on the ground, it became obvious he was unmistakably alone. It wasn't much longer before he finally reached the hills.

He looked for a path, a trail, something to get him higher. He did spot an area that looked like it might offer some support so he could climb up the side of the hill, a series of outcroppings almost like stairs, only less uniform, obviously naturally formed.

He ascended twenty or thirty feet before looking down and vertigo struck like a sucker punch. He closed his eyes and hugged the hillside, then shifted his focus above, concentrating only on reaching the top.

As he made his way up, he tried once again to plumb his memory. Something in there had to make sense. How long had he been here, wherever here was? What was his last memory? Again, it wasn't a matter of not having the memory there. He could see images in his mind, but he couldn't put the names to any of them. He saw faces of people he knew, but whose place in his life he couldn't recall. He saw places, objects, events, but none of it had a name, just pictures.

He was almost at the top of the hill when he ran out of footholds.

He dared another look down only to gauge how secure was his current footing, and whether there was anywhere else to go from here that might aid in reaching the top. He saw an outcropping and found it to be within reach, so he grabbed it and swung his weight over to it. Then he used it to haul himself up to the top of the hill where he could look out over the wasteland and, hopefully, figure out where he was.

Looking back over the distance he'd covered to get here, any hope he'd had sank immediately. There was nothing. Desert. That sluggish lake. Nothing else. As far as he could see there was only sun-blasted wasteland.

He turned around, hoping for something else on the other side of the hills, fearful it would be more of the same. He certainly did not expect to find the remains of a crashed alien ship.

He stared at it, trying to form the word in his mind, "ship", but his language was gone and all he had was this image. He knew very well what it was, but his mind was still resistant.

To reach it he would have to climb back down the mountain. He tried to judge its distance, but with nothing behind it but more desert, there was nothing to judge it in relation to. He went to the edge of the hill again and started his descent.

The way down was easier, but more treacherous and he had to go even slower to avoid being caught in a slide and losing control. By the time he reached the desert floor again, his arms throbbed and his muscles flared with red hot pain.

His focus was just as off as his balance, but he finally got to his feet again, steadied himself, and headed for the ship. He stumbled. He had to course correct several times. He looked up at the sun, trying to figure out how long he'd been out here. Nothing worked in his mind. Every word he wanted to form was right on the tip of his tongue, but even that, tongue, was a word that escaped him.

As he walked he looked down at his hands and tried to form that word. He swept back the hair plastered to his forehead, tried to recall that word, and couldn't. He even knew it started with the same letter as hands. It was a word he could say with a simple exhale, but he was broken and could only walk dumbly on.

He felt a great despair settle around as reality overwhelmed him. Alone in the desert with no one, no memory, not even the ability to think.

The ship grew larger and larger as he stumbled along. It really was massive, he realized. His legs were about to give out, but he kept moving from nothing more than the fear of lying helpless in the middle of the desert with that sun beating down on him. It kept him moving, but just barely.

He finally reached the ship,

He touched its surface, hesitantly. The sun had warmed the metal so it burned and he drew his hand away quickly. He took in as much detail as he could, marveling at shafts, intakes, vents, a half dozen other features he wouldn't have imagined. He followed a series of ladders down the line of the ship, around what was now the underside—it appeared to have crashed nearly on its side, and at an angle so the rear of the ship was several yards off the ground—to a hatch.

Would it open? Was there something inside?

The latch looked like nothing more complicated than a handle which he could turn and, presumably, unlock the door. He grabbed the handle. On this side of the ship, in the shadows, the metal was cool and thick. He thought of old railroad cars near his grandmother's house as a boy, and this memory sparked a hope in him, but still no matter how he fought for the words, nothing came. It was all just pictures, memories without substance.

He gripped the latch and turned it. The mechanism screeched as metal slid against metal, but it moved. The door popped outward with a tiny hiss and he was able to pull the door open.

A cool breeze blew out at him and the sweat on his forehead vanished.

He moved closer, waiting for whatever would attack to do so.

Nothing happened.

He lifted himself up into the ship, which wasn't easy with the angle at which it had touched down. It reminded him of a funhouse he'd visited once where the floor went progressively more crooked the further he went. The door beeped, clicked, then slid shut again behind him. The lock engaged and he fell back, anxious, terrified.

The ship was black. Its walls hummed with secret life, but it was just the electrical systems talking to each other. He detected no alien chatter from some hidden inner room. No ray guns revved to life, ready to blast him to ash.

The air tasted different in here. It was sweeter for sure. The desert air he realized now had been burning his lungs very slightly.

He felt like a kitten approaching a sleeping puppy, moving forward into uncertain territory. Feeling his way in the dark, he moved up past a column with sharp edges, around a series of cubbies and mesh panels, then to a ladder attached to a wall. He held tight to the rungs, gravity at his back at this angle, and climbed the ladder to a hole in the ceiling, then up into a second level of the ship. He braced himself in the dark, got to his feet, and tried to look around. The darkness was too absolute, though.

"Lights," he said, amazed that the word had come to him.

The ship beeped and flashed to life as the room lit up with hundreds of dials and monitors, plus an overhead light that showed him the cockpit of the ship.

He looked around, still very cautious. The cockpit seemed standard, not alien at all. He didn't know what he'd been expecting but it wasn't two leather seats up front with an array of controls and dials. It looked way too human, is what he thought.

He looked at the switches, wondering if he'd be able to piece together how to operate this thing. He wasn't even sure it could be operated, but the electrical still worked, so he had to hope the rest did as well.

Right now, he had another concern. His body would give out in about five minutes if he didn't get, "Food."

He said the word as easily as anything, as if he'd never forgotten it. But where would he find food on an alien ship?

This level, two sections back.

How did he know that? Had he been abducted by the ship's occupants? Maybe in the crash, he'd been thrown out and wound up miles away in the water?

It seemed implausible to have been thrown that great a distance and not broken anything, even if he landed in the water. It couldn't be that simple.

And maybe, he decided, he'd be able to think a little more clearly if he ate. That is, if this ship contained anything he *could* eat.

Two sections back, past a computer room and a storage area, he found a small, enclosed kitchen.

The angle of the ship was making getting anywhere more difficult the longer he was subject to their extremes, and his weakening body wasn't his friend. He closed the panel door behind him, thinking if gravity overcame him, at least he wouldn't tumble out of the room and hurt himself. Certainly, the further he got toward the rear to the ship, the more dangerous and vertiginous the angle seemed.

He went immediately to a cupboard and pulled out a box of dehydrated fruit chips, tore them open and stuffed his mouth with them. He didn't question the contents, just recognized their heavenly smell and knew they would be good.

He set them down and went to the water tank, sucked greedily at it, then realized he'd overdone it and tried not to throw it all back up.

Then his actions hit him and he asked, "How did I know this was here?"

He was elated his language skills had returned, but the memories were still shrouded in a purple haze and it made him very uncomfortable being in this place, apparently familiar enough with it, but not knowing why.

He looked around at the room, getting the details, trying to see if any of them sparked a memory. Then he went further back in the ship, to the next section, which was a hallway with several panel doors along each side. Two closets, two lavatories.

Up another level would be an exercise room and living spaces. They lived up on the next level in small apartments. And below were computers and all the equipment needed to run the ship. Recycling centers for water, the oxygen tanks as well as the gardens which sprouted thick and green, giving them plenty of breathable air so their tanks weren't depleted before the end of their mission.

He found a ladder and climbed up to the next level. The details came back, but the memories still refused to surface. He knew too much about this ship, especially considering he still didn't know *how* he knew. As far as he was concerned, seeing it from the hilltop had been his first encounter with it. And he still wasn't sure whatever aliens had crashed it here weren't around somewhere, maybe hiding, or injured.

He shivered in the cool air from the sweat on his back. He knew if anything attacked him, he was defenseless and weak, so as he moved through the corridors he looked for weapons. Even though he knew if he wanted real weapons they were stored in the front compartment of the top level. Again, how did he know?

He found a door and knew the person who slept here had blonde hair.

He opened the door and slid through into the room. It was tidy, sparse, and definitely belonged to a girl.

"Elaina," he said. His daughter.

The word stopped him and he looked around, suddenly sure he was being watched. He said the name again, louder, calling for her. He received no reply. He climbed out of the room and went into the next room, calling "Thomas! Thomas!" But his son never replied. Back in the hall he took two deep inhalations of fresh, crisp oxygen and yelled, "Where is everyone?"

The ship remained silent save his panting and the hum of electricity.

He checked the other compartments, even though he knew what he would find—or rather, what he wouldn't find.

The ship was deserted. Where had they gone? He'd been outside when he woke up. He still couldn't remember why. He was just there. They were probably out there too, then. But where?

He climbed down to the main level again and made his way forward to the cockpit. While the computers worked, the engine was dead. The diagnostic revealed irreparable damage sustained in the landing.

He checked the logs. The computer showed his entries for the last month, but he didn't bother going back any further. The last entry had been made ten days ago as they approached the planet.

"Planet?"

The log of their approach showed a planet slightly larger than earth, mostly desert, probably uninhabited. The air was breathable, although higher in nitrous oxide than oxygen.

He went forward, but that last entry from a week and a half ago showed them all getting ready to disembark in exploration.

The oxygen levels weren't ideal, but manageable, so they left the suits and tanks in storage. That was the last he'd seen of his family and it was only as he watched the recording that the memories of that day finally started to come back.

Elaina and Thomas were excited, but his wife, Clea, was even more so. They'd been so long in isolation on the ship, she just wanted to get out and breathe and walk and be free. To be safe, they all went together, in the same direction. Toward the hills, because in all the other directions visible from the ship, there was nothing but sand and sun. So they went toward the only unknown thing they found.

Now it was a week and a half later and he didn't know what had happened to them.

He had to find them.

Panicked, he struggled back to the kitchen, shoved his pockets full of fruit chips, shoved two bottles of water in his pockets—all they would hold—and climbed back down. He wondered for a second if he should get a rifle, but he'd been out there for how many hours wandering back to the ship and hadn't seen a thing.

The only danger out there was exposure, and the rifles would do nothing against that. He opened the hatch and leapt out onto the dusty ground, back into the unforgiving heat. The door beeped, clicked, and slid shut again behind him.

He wound around the crashed nose of the ship and headed for the hills. He wanted to run, but knew he had to keep his strength up and preserve what little energy the fruit chips had given him. He would get there, but his wife and children wouldn't be helped at all if he killed himself before he could reach them.

The walk back to the hill didn't seem to take as long although he had to stop twice and sit down for a moment; he wasn't wearing himself out, but he still had severe moments of lightheadedness. And when that turned to dizziness, he knew he had to rest.

He had a mission. The sun was so hot, though. So bright. He wanted to close his eyes.

At the foot of the hills he drank a bottle of water, energizing himself for the climb. But at the top of the hill he'd forgotten, and he drank the other bottle.

He stood on the hill, looking out into the distance. He saw nothing in that direction for a minute. Then, as he continued scanning the horizon he saw a shimmer. He'd taken it for heat shimmer, but when he really focused it looked like water. He could use some water.

It was so hot. He went carefully down the side of the hill, spilling dried fruit chips from his pocket, skidding and sliding, but he never fell.

It was close once and he looked around nervously as people do when they find themselves in a clumsy position, then he reminded himself there was no one to laugh at him. He was alone. He was fine.

At the bottom he walked forward several yards, trying to remember exactly where that heat shimmer had been. There was something there he wanted to find. Something . . . what was the word . . . something cool, something wet . . . he couldn't remember off the top of his head, but he could see it. He wanted it. He was burning up out here.

Where was he, anyway? He'd worry about that later. He needed to get to that . . . stuff, whatever it was called. He walked on and the heat bore down, the sun blinding and the haze setting in. He felt like he wanted to call out to someone, and a face appeared briefly in his memory, then it evaporated into nothing. There was a name on the tip of his tongue. The tip of his . . . what was it? He moved it in his mouth, but couldn't say its name. The tip . . . the . . . where was he?

He couldn't wait to reach that thing up there. The wet thing. The cool thing. What was it called? God, he was hot.

Write a story in which someone is killed by unusual means, for example a comb, a sock, or a bar of soap.

OBSESSIVE COMPULSIVE DISMEMBERMENT

(originally published in Scared Naked*)*

• • • •

GRADY WAS IN THE BATHROOM, grabbing everything he'd need, tweezers, plastic bags, his cup. He was reaching for the soap when the phone rang. He stood beside it until it rang a second time, then a third. If whoever was on the other end knew him at all, they'd hang up and call again. If there was a fourth ring, he didn't know them, and he wouldn't answer.

The phone was silent a good ten seconds. Then it rang again. On the third ring, he picked up.

"Hello? . . . I'm getting ready to leave . . . Just out for a while . . . I don't know, later. Yeah, okay. I'll call you then. Love you, too. Bye."

He hung up, picked his bag off the floor beside him, grabbed his keys from the hook by the door, and was gone before his mother could call back.

He locked the door, put the keys in his pocket, patted his pocket to make sure the keys had gone to the bottom and hadn't fallen out as soon as he let go of them, and the walked to the stairs. His mother's call must have distracted him more than he thought because he reached the stairs, ready to step down with the wrong foot. He walked back to the door, took the keys out of his pocket, unlocked, then re-locked the door, stuffed the keys into his pocket—patting the pocket to make sure the keys had gone to the bottom—and walked to the stairs again, this time arriving with the correct foot. He stepped down onto the first step with his left, reached the bottom on his right, and was out the front door three steps later.

He'd gone left last time, so tonight he would go right.

He passed the adult bookstore, glanced in and counted the racks: one, two, three, then the wall. He passed the coffee shop, glanced in, counted the booths: one, two, three, four. Now his rhythm was off and he'd have to walk until he found a business with either two to make up for the extra booth, or five to get to the next set. It was a struggle to keep his eyes off the outside wall of the theater; it had only one movie poster. There was a bar up ahead. It had two windows. And the gas station after that had two pumps. If he was quick, before he passed it and lost the chance—.

He glanced at the movie poster, counted it as one, then went on, looking for the bar and the gas station to keep him on track and get to twelve.

With all this trouble staying on track, Grady could already tell the night was going to be a rough one.

• • • •

HE'D BEEN MAKING HIS way through the buildings three at a time, but then he realized that was a predictable pattern for anyone to discover, so he started working backward, counting the one before his last one as one, and going to them by threes from there. It was a difficult pattern to see, he knew, unless he showed it to someone, and that made him even more comfortable with it. It made sense to him, and if, in the process, it kept everyone else off track, all the better. However, he couldn't always remember which was next, so he sometimes ended up walking four miles out of his way—after all, it wasn't like the buildings were placed right next to each other—and then backtracking, keeping count as he went.

It was almost midnight before he made his way back down the street to the building he was going to. The address was 571. All prime numbers, and all odd. No way to divide that one in half. Nor were any of them multiples of three. It was bad enough they were prime *and* odd, but at least if he could divide them by three, he would have been more comfortable with things. He had a bad feeling about this one.

He went up the steps, opened the door—thank God for the landlords too cheap to install the security locks—and looked at the mailboxes.

Siddons in 2 would have been a possibility if not for that final "s" throwing everything out of symmetry. There was a Possop in 5, but palindromes had never proved to be easy for him. They felt wrong from the moment he saw the names. All he needed was a good, even-lettered name. Here was Walker. Looks like we have a winner, he thought. And it was his third choice. Even better. Maybe the address wouldn't prove to be such a hindrance after all.

Walker was in 7, on the second floor.

Grady went upstairs, stopped outside Walker's door, and prepared.

He knocked and heard a voice inside say, "Who the hell is knocking at this time of night?" There was a pause, movement toward the door that Grady discerned through the floorboards in the apartment creaking, and then the voice asked, "Who the hell is it?"

"Mr. Walker?"

"Who's asking?"

"Sir, I need you to open the door, please."

"Who is it? The police? What do you want?"

"Sir, I need you to open the door, please," Grady repeated.

There was a sigh, then the unlocking of several locks. Grady only counted four, and he kept waiting for more to even it out, but he knew that would be an awful lot of locks because he couldn't stop on six, either. It was three or nine at *least*. Nothing in between. On rare occasions five would do, but with the building numbers so bad already, and Walker being in apartment 7, he'd need three or nine to put him at ease. The four was all he got. He'd just make sure to lock and unlock them enough times from the inside to make up for it.

The door came open a crack and Grady kicked it in, stepped inside, then closed it again with his foot.

Walker . . . wasn't where Grady'd expected him.

There he was . . . three feet below where Grady was looking . . . in a wheelchair.

"What the hell is all this happy horseshit?" Walker asked, looking up at the crazy man.

"Shh," Grady said. He slapped a piece of tape over the man's mouth, then punched him in the face. Walker went out like a light.

Grady turned back to the door, locked and unlocked the doors until a pleasing pattern had been achieved. And then he turned back to Walker.

• • • •

FOR GRADY, THE JOY was in the doing.

He went into Walker's bedroom, stripped the sheet off, and spread it across the living room floor. He took the unconscious man out of the wheelchair and laid him flat. He taped Walker's wrists together. He straddled the crippled man's chest, then leaned over his face. He tapped Walker in the head, whispering, "Wake up, Mr. Walker."

Walker's eyes fluttered and he moaned through the tape. Then he came to, saw the man over him, and tried to scream. The tape kept him muffled.

When Walker was fully awake, Grady stabbed him in the throat.

The planning was just so much consideration and finding the patterns in things, enough to keep him at ease. But when he was killing, he was free. Free of the patterns and the numbers and the symmetry, and he could finally breathe easy.

When he was dissecting, he wasn't concerned with how many fingers he took off, or how many inches long was the length of intestine he wrapped around the victim's neck. He didn't have to abide by any patterns when it came to scooping someone's eyeballs out. If he felt like grabbing the right one first, it didn't matter if he'd taken the right one first last time. When he broke off someone's teeth, they didn't have to be removed in a symmetrical pattern. And when he was standing over the ruined corpse, masturbating into his collection cup, he didn't have to count the strokes to make sure he ended on a multiple of three.

When Grady was killing, it was the only time he was able to just be. So he did it as often as he could manage.

Grady came into his cup, put the lid on, wrapped tape around it so the lid didn't pop off and spill semen all over the place, then put the cup into his bag. He got the tweezers from his bag, next, and crawled around the body, grabbing any hairs he saw, because he never knew if one of them might be his.

When the sheet was clean of everything except the dead Mr. Walker and Mr. Walker's remnants, Grady went back into his bag to get his soap.

He moved aside the spare gloves, the roll of tape. The soap wasn't under his spool of fishing line. And he didn't find it behind the ball gag.

Then he remembered his mother calling right before he grabbed the fresh box with the unused bar out of his cabinet.

Shit.

This couldn't be happening. Grady was always so careful, how could he have let something like a bar of soap slip his mind? All he had to do was grab it, then go listen for the fourth ring, whether it came or not. He knew he wasn't going to pick up the phone right then, so why the hell did he stop what he was doing and go wait by it? Now he didn't have his soap, and God knew if this guy would have the stuff he needed.

Could he even use someone else's soap? He wasn't sure. It had never come up before. But now that it had, would his DNA be able to be tracked back to him through a bar of soap?

Granted, he ran that chance every time he used his own soap; with Grady's skin condition, he had to rely on a few specific soaps, stuff the common man in the city wouldn't have. If the police ever realized that, it wouldn't take too very long to track it back to Grady. After all, there couldn't have been more than a few dozen people in the city who'd even heard of his soap.

Surely, the chances of Mr. Walker here knowing about it were slim and none.

But Grady had to wash up. There was no way around that fact. Not only did killing allow him the chance to act regardless of patterns and numbers, it also allowed him to get dirty. He always had to wash up afterward. It was either that, or get caught the second he stepped out of the door.

He got a large square of cheesecloth from his bag, spread it over the shower drain, and then weighed the side down with whatever he could find. The cloth would catch any stray hairs before they went down the drain.

Grady stripped, folded his clothes neatly, laid them on the toilet seat lid, then climbed into the shower.

He sniffed the soap before picking it up. It didn't smell too bad. It was only a half bar, so the original shape was gone, and the original color had been melted and worn down to a light green. Well, that shouldn't be too bad. There were a number of soaps he shouldn't use, but only three he absolutely could not use. And they were all white.

He wasn't crazy about the thought of using someone else's soap. It was too much like using their toothbrush. God knew where Mr. Walker'd had this thing.

He picked it up, scrubbed thoroughly, but as quickly as possible, and set the bar back in its tray. He rinsed and inspected his body. He found no signs of blood spatter. The cheesecloth was pink now.

He turned off the shower, folded the ends of the cloth over each other, slipped it into a plastic bag, and dried off. He would take the towel with him, burn it in the incinerator at his building.

Grady was looking at himself in the mirror to make sure he really had washed off all the blood, when his glance shifted down for just a second, into the trash can beside Mr. Walker's toilet.

"What's this?" he asked.

He leaned over, stared at the box, and had to turn his head upside down to read the label. NEW PINE GREEN SCENT, the box announced. But the name of the soap . . . Grady couldn't believe how utterly wrong his luck had been tonight. Of all the soaps in the world for Mr. Walker to use, it would be one of the three he could not use, now in green.

Grady felt the burning in his skin almost immediately after his realization.

He looked in the mirror and saw his skin turning red, blisters breaking out in a rash all over him. His face was like one huge sack of pus, ready to burst. He rubbed his eyes, trying to make the vision go away, but there must have been soap on his hands still because then his eyes burned, and then he couldn't see anymore because of the blisters forming on his eyeballs.

He thrashed around the bathroom, trying to get past the pain of his entire body revolting over one stupid mistake like the wrong soap.

He bit his lip while fighting back his screams, but that only made him rub the bleeding lip, and from there it was all over in seconds. The poison got into his mouth and formed blisters, it got into his blood and ran to his entire body and formed blisters, from his eyes and mouth both it got to his brain and formed blisters.

Grady was dead three minutes after he collapsed on the bathroom floor. He knew it took that long, because all he could do while he lay there dying was count. He got to one hundred eighty before he blacked out.

Rewrite a familiar fairy tale from an unexpected point of view.

LUCK OF THE DRAW

(originally published in Horror Carousel*)*

. . . .

JOHN, AS WHAT PASSED for sheriff in the little German village, was in charge of the annual lottery, which would be held tomorrow after Sunday service. The children would be outside playing in the sun while the parents sat inside in grim silence.

Life in their village was, as far as John could tell, about as close to perfect as one was likely to find. The farmers worked together to make sure everyone had food, the business owners worked together to make sure anything that couldn't be grown or made within the community was brought in from outside, the families worked together to make sure the children were cared for. John had once heard a phrase about it taking a village to raise a child and he supposed that was true. For the most part the village acted as a one. But that's what a secret does, isn't it, John thought. It brings people together in the keeping and suffering of it.

He took a large burlap sack from a trunk he kept out of sight all the rest of the year so he didn't have to think about the cost of survival in their hidden corner of the world. He unfolded the bag, made sure rats hadn't gotten into the trunk and chewed holes in it, and was about to hang it on the door. Before he could turn around, a hand, wet and stinking, covered his mouth while something sharp poked him in the throat.

The smell of the flesh made his stomach roll and John felt the stew he'd had for supper coming back up. The skin was covered in something sticky that greased John's face. He would have that smell on him for days, he thought. The thing sticking in his neck was nothing compared to that reek.

John didn't have to wonder who, only why. They were sticking to the deal, he would have said if he could, they were going to make their payment in eight days. But when the voice whispered in his ear, he knew this year, and most likely all the years to follow, things weren't going to be that easy. As if the lottery were ever easy. But this year it would be twice as difficult.

Then she was gone again just as quickly as she'd come, vanishing into the shadows like the monster she was.

John looked at the sack hanging on his door and thought of the black day that would follow. Yes, the community worked together for the betterment of all, but there was that time each year when one family was set aside from the others, when everyone in town sighed and resumed their good lives, knowing the shadow cast by the thing in the forest was falling on one of their own, helpless to stop it, but content that it hadn't fallen on them.

. . . .

NO TIME WAS WASTED the next day. The final prayer given, the children sent outside with the pastor who kept them entertained, knowing what was going on inside and damning the people each year for allowing it. But what else could they do? The bag was passed around. Each family dropped in their placards and John took the bag to the head of the church. Standing in front of the alter, he gave the bag a shake. The placards inside clinked against one another, and everyone knew it was destiny clacking for one of them. Without looking at any them—he still hadn't given them the news—he reached his hand inside, dug around the placards, and pulled one out.

He read the name, which was immediately followed by the wailing he knew was coming. He tried not to notice the look of relief on the faces of the other families. Unmarried and childless, John's regret at having to go through with this every year was knowing he would have to face the families later on, knowing it was his hand that had settled on that placard, his that had chosen which of their children to send to its death in the forest. And if things weren't bad enough. . . .

"I have to make an announcement," he said before anyone could retreat, lucky and thankful at having escaped their own child's name being read for another year.

Everyone sat and looked at him, wondering what could be the news. This had never happened before, keeping everyone there. The general rule was the name was read, a moment was given for it to sink in, and everyone left as soon as possible. It was really best for everyone, this pattern. But now this new twist.

"I, um," John stammered, trying to force himself to get on with it. "I received a visit last night," he finally told them. Everyone looked around. Everyone except Wilhelm and his wife, holding each other and crying. "She came to me last night."

This was news, and nothing that could be good. The lottery was held as usual, so they knew it hadn't been called off. But she'd come out of the forest for something. What was it?

"She wants two this year," John said.

The church gasped as one. They searched his face for a lie, but found none.

Without another word, he shook the bag again and reached in for another name.

When he pulled it out and looked at it, John felt his heart sink and his stomach turned to fire. In a voice that cracked with his regret, he read the name and set the placard down next to the other one. He looked at them a second, two names, a boy and a girl, brother and sister, their parents losing both children at once.

He couldn't imagine what was going through their heads, but he knew the thoughts in his own were bad enough to make him go home and thank the Lord he hadn't any children of his own whose names might one day be drawn from the sack.

• • • •

WITHIN FIVE HOURS OF the drawing that day, John was too drunk to stand. He spent the next three days in a similar state, knowing it didn't matter, that by week's end, no matter how he'd tried to forget, he'd be sitting alone in front of his fire, wiping away tears and praying to forget while two innocent children were led into the forest as sacrifice for the sake of the village.

He almost got his gun and strode into the forest himself, meaning to kill the witch and be done with it, but John, like everyone else in the village, had grown up with her legend to keep them at bay, the stories of what she'd done to the few brave enough to stand against her and how they'd never lived to make another bad decision again. The stories also said none of those unfortunates had died quickly enough. The witch's powers stretched far. She didn't have to come into town to make them pay. Those few suffered enough in a short time to make sure no one else ever tried to prevent the witch from collecting her fee for leaving them in peace the rest of the year.

Before he could lay a hand on his rifle, he thought of these stories. He knew it would be a long time before he could face Wilhelm again, but he knew eventually he could and they would both know it wasn't John's decision, simply the luck of the draw. He knew one day Wilhelm and his wife would forgive him. He could live with that. Besides, he'd carried this burden ten years or more already. John knew he couldn't live forever. What was one more burden on top of the others when surely there weren't many years left anyway.?

That decision didn't change his behavior, though, and he remained drunk and secluded in his house the rest of the week. On Sunday, he skipped service.

He always did on the day of the sacrifice.

It wasn't bad enough she demanded one of their children—two of their children now—she had to do on the Lord's day while everyone else prayed and pretended they were going to Heaven? On that day, he lit the fire, settled in front of it with his jug, and watched the flames dance.

He thought of nothing for hours, just watched the colors change and drank himself into a moaning stupor, eventually crying and wishing the world would end because any world that demanded of someone what he'd been forced to do over and over couldn't be one that was good for anything at all.

Near midnight, he finally stood up.

His breeches were soaked with piss and spilled booze.

John dropped his jug and took his rifle down from the wall. He went back to his chair and sat in front of the fire again, the iron having replaced the clay in his grasp.

He'd made his decision finally. The witch would never let them go. She'd been tormenting them before John was born and would be here still when he was gone. He would never see the day when their village was free of her. When that truth made itself crystal clear to his admittedly muddled mind, he knew he couldn't see another family ruined because of the reach of John's fingers. And now it would be two because what were the chances he'd ever again draw two names from one family in the same day? No, that wasn't something he could be a part of any longer. The village would go on, they'd vote another sheriff and the heartbreak and guilt would be their problem, not John's, not any longer.

He put the barrel of his rifle to his chin, said a prayer, and placed his finger on the trigger, ready to push and fire.

The door burst open and one of the men from the village, Jakob, fell inside yelling, "John, come quick. They're back. The children."

John dropped the gun and moved away from it, hoping to hide what he'd been about to do. He stepped into the shadows and wiped at his face, trying to clear his head for just a second and make sense of what Jakob had just said.

"What?" he asked. "What do you mean?"

"I mean they've come back, the children. Wilhelm sent them off this morning, and then tonight, just an hour ago, they came back, said they'd done her in, tricked her into cooking herself, the girl did."

John took a breathe. There are few moments in life where one feels their world changing, but this was one of those few.

"They're back?" he asked.

"Yes."

"Hansel?"

"And Grethel, as well," the other man said. "Come on, we're gathering everyone in the church to make the announcement. Then we're going to send a team into the forest to make sure"

"And if they're wrong and she's still there?"

"John, the children have come back. That's never happened."

John felt his tears start again, this time though for different reasons and he let them come.

"Give me a minute," he said. "I'll meet you there."

"Hurry," Jakob said, and ran off to spread the news.

John closed the door against the night, went back to his chair and stared at the rifle lying on the floor.

He picked it up, hung it back on its hook on the wall. Then he sat in his chair again and cried some more, now in big heaving sobs, wondering how the world could work like this, and was it really the luck of the draw that had brought it on, was it really only a matter of John's own clumsy hands that brought everything together, the perfect piece to make this puzzle complete?

He didn't know.

He might never understand.

But he knew one thing, there was a family he had to face. There was a man to congratulate, and two children to hug as if they were his own.

Rewrite your favorite movie. Obviously you don't want to rewrite it beat for beat, but use that movie as the inspiration for your own take on a similar subject. For me, it's always been THE EXORCIST. There are so many facets of that movie that intrigue me as a horror writer. So I came up with this:

THE PRISONER

• • • •

PETER HAD LAIN AWAKE for a while, drifting in and out of the world, never sleeping, but not always conscious, either. It was the cat that brought him back. As soon as it squealed and squawked, then went silent, he remembered, vaguely, having heard it whining in heat earlier in the evening. It was only when he stopped to think about it that he realized it must have been crying all night. And then finally the thing in the back room had tired of its noise and had silenced it. Easy as that.

Like it did Susan, Peter thought. Only a cat was much easier to explain away than a dead wife. At first he was suspected. He'd found her, after all. No one had been home except Peter, Susan, and . . . he'd almost said Daniel. But Daniel had been gone a good month by then, although no one knew it. They still didn't, in fact. Peter had come to believe the only reason the police had finally accepted her death as an accident was because the thing in the back room upstairs had made them. It still needed Peter to feed it, which he couldn't do if he was locked away. And if Peter was gone, someone would come in and take . . . not Daniel, he thought, the *thing*, and if they did that, it wouldn't take a genius to realize something was wrong with him. One look would do it.

And then what? The thing knew if it was discovered, there'd be steps taken to get rid of it. And what good would that do it?

So Peter was cleared, Susan was buried, and the thing continued to torment Daniel's father.

Now the cat. Susan was easy, the thing's influence within the house was well-established. But now it could reach outside the house as well.

How far, Peter wondered. And what would it do with that reach? Was there something out there it wanted? Why not send Peter to bring it back? Because it was afraid if he got outside he'd never come back?

The thing was tormenting his *son*, Peter would never abandon Daniel like that.

But whatever it wanted, any time he'd asked—always in frustration—the thing only laughed and said, "Wait." Peter only prayed that whenever it got what it had come for, it would leave and let Daniel alone for good.

He felt eyes on his back, and he turned over in his bed to face the stare. But the room was empty.

He still hadn't got used to being in the bed alone, even though Susan had been in the ground three weeks already. In fact, lying in bed was the hardest part of Peter's day. During the morning, afternoon, and evening, he spent his time taking care of Daniel (not the thing, he thought, he wasn't caring for the thing, only Daniel), and didn't have time to stop and think of anything. It was only at night, in bed, unable to sleep, that all the thoughts he didn't have in the daytime came rushing at him. It was then he felt most helpless, most alone, and most terrified.

It was also when he felt the most angry. Every second he had to see his son twisted and broken into an image more closely resembling the thing inside him was agony for Peter and he wished he could drag it screaming from his son and then beat it to death with a baseball bat before feeding it to a pack of wolves. But that hatred was nothing compared to what he felt lying alone in his bed at night with the house finally quiet around him, the thing down the hall resting. At those times, he knew a bat wouldn't be good enough, he'd have to beat it to death with a cinder block, cave in its rotten head, run it over with a bus, tear the remains to pieces with his bare hands, and burn the segments with acid.

But in reality all he could do was wait, see what it wanted, and try to keep his mind intact until then.

• • • •

IF ASKED TWO MONTHS ago Peter's opinions on heaven and hell, he'd have given a short answer. He'd have shrugged and said "Don't know. I'll find out sooner or later, I suppose." If asked his opinions on angels and demons, he'd have shaken his head and given a solid, "No such thing. Even if the places up and down are real, I doubt it's where the angels and demons live." If asked why he could possibly believe in places like heaven and hell but dismiss angels and demons, he wouldn't have been able to answer. This wasn't a topic Peter ever gave much thought. Like he would have said, if asked, he would find out sooner or later. Until then, he figured, he had real things to worry about, like trying to remember to mail the house payment, like the good two hours overtime he was going to have to work tomorrow if he hoped to avoid working the weekend, like Daniel sitting at one end of the couch, whining that his head hurt.

Peter never got headaches, and he knew kids could sometimes exaggerate their pains, so he gave his son two aspirin and told him it would go away "in a little bit."

If asked, Peter would have said, "No, it's just a headache," and left it at that.

In the morning, the headache was still there. By afternoon, a stomachache had joined it. By that night, Daniel was shitting blood.

Susan took him to the emergency room while Daniel was just getting home from work, showering, and grabbing something to eat. He would meet them out there if they were still there an hour later. On the drive out, he berated himself for downplaying Daniel's pain.

"He's just a kid," he told himself. "You can't tell, you should have listened to him, whether it turned out to be nothing or something, either way."

But how could he have known? He couldn't. Peter thought this was the biggest difference between adults and children, and the scariest thing about raising them; you could just never tell when they were really hurt, or how serious it was.

He was only a few blocks from the hospital when Susan called him. "Where are you?"

"I'm almost there," he said. "How is he?"

"We're leaving now," she said. "The doctor gave him a shot and a prescription, said it was probably just the flu."

"I've had the flu," Peter said, "I've never shat blood."

"Well, they're the ones supposed to know these things."

"Okay, I'm gonna turn around then, I'll meet you back at home."

"All right."

"Tell him I love him," Peter said.

They brought Daniel home, put him to bed and sat beside him while he cried himself to sleep that night, Peter and Susan helpless, knowing that although he was in pain, if he could fall asleep, it would stop for a few hours. All he needed was some rest and in the morning he would probably feel a lot better.

The next day, he said his stomach and head still hurt, but he stopped shitting blood. That was a good sign, until he started vomiting. He'd eaten very little and most of what came up was green and burning, a pool of stomach acid, the last of it dripping from Daniel's open mouth in a thin string of spit.

He wiped it away, crawled back to bed, and hadn't been out of it since.

Susan fed him his antibiotics, kept him hydrated, and waited for the flu to work through its cycle. It would still be another two weeks before either of them admitted that what was wrong with their son was more than a virus. Peter was the hardest sell; heaven and hell might be real, but it wasn't where the angels and demons lived, because there was no such thing.

Then the thing in the back room started playing with them and they had to stop and look at the situation, impossible and horrifying as it was.

· · · ·

SUSAN WAS WALKING UP the stairs, bringing Daniel his lunch. He'd been eating a little more in the last couple of days and Susan hoped keeping his strength up might help fight the infection.

She'd reached the top of the stairs when the phone rang. She'd been waiting for a call from Daniel's doctor, hoping he might have some advice, or maybe be able to call in a stronger prescription because the antibiotics weren't helping.

She jumped when the phone rang and jostled the soup bowl, some splashed over the lip. She set the bowl at the top of the stairs and ran down to grab the phone.

When she picked it up, the line was dead. She shrugged, hung it up, and went back up the stairs. She had the bowl in hand when the phone rang again. She ran down again, hoping to get it before they hung up this time, but when she put it to her ear, there was only the dial tone.

In the few seconds she stood there, she heard Daniel upstairs laughing.

He's feeling a little better at least, she thought.

She grabbed the phone off the base and carried it up with her. If Daniel's doctor was trying to call, she'd be sure to get it next time.

She took Daniel his soup and sat on the edge of the bed, spooning it into his mouth.

He was chuckling between bites and his eyes kept going to the phone sitting next to Susan.

"I take it you're better today?" she asked. "What's so funny."

Before he could answer, the phone rang again.

"Hang on," she said, "that might be the doctor."

There was no one there again.

Daniel was laughing now. It was infectious and soon Susan was giggling along with him.

"What's so funny?" she asked.

The phone rang again. By this time, Susan was no longer so concerned with the doctor calling and more interested that whoever *was* calling stop.

"Hello?" she said with a bit of frustration.

The line was dead.

Daniel was cackling now.

"Daniel, you're gonna make yourself sick if you don't calm down."

At that the laughter stopped, as if on a switch, and Daniel sat up in bed, his face was straight and his eyes empty. He looked first at Susan, then at the phone.

It rang. She let it ring twice before putting it to her ear, her eyes never leaving her son who was now staring at her again.

She clicked the phone to ON and brought it to her ear, slowly, knowing now that something was wrong, it was in the look on Daniel's face. The dial tone was replaced by static now.

Daniel had gone back to giggling.

She turned off the phone, set it on the bed.

She was still watching Daniel when it rang again.

He stopped laughing and watched her.

When she brought the phone to her ear this time, she asked, "Hello?", then dropped it, nearly threw it away from her, when she heard Daniel's voice on the other end.

"Where are you, Mom?" he asked. "I can't find you."

His voice was thin and distant, as if he were very small in a big empty room.

Susan stood up and backed away from the bed.

The boy on the bed was still watching her, not laughing now, but smiling. There was no humor in that grin. She got to the bottom of the stairs, then somehow managed to make it into the kitchen before throwing up in the sink. Her stomach was rolling and her heart said if she didn't do something soon it was going to explode. She rinsed her mouth with water, then drank some, and sat on the kitchen floor holding her head in her hands, trying not to cry, and wondering for the first time what was going on.

She'd known the prescription wasn't helping, she'd known Daniel, despite his good days when he had them, wasn't getting any better, not really, but whatever was wrong with him, it was something besides the flu. That was obvious now, because what just happened up there, that doesn't happen, not in the real world. She couldn't explain it, but she also couldn't deny it.

The phone rang again. She could hear it, ringing where she'd tossed it, along the wall in Daniel's room upstairs, but the door was open and the house was otherwise quiet and the noise traveled to her clearly. It rang for fifteen minutes before it stopped.

When it rang again ten minutes later, she unplugged the base from the wall, which should have silenced the noise, but it went on.

When Peter came home, he found her outside, three houses down, sitting on the sidewalk with her knees drawn up and her hands over her ears.

It took half an hour to coax her back into the house, another half hour before she could tell him what had happened. As soon as she finished her story, Peter went upstairs to check on Daniel. He was asleep.

When he came back down, he said, "He's fine now. I didn't see the—." But before he could say "phone", he spotted it on the base where it belonged. "Here it is," he said.

Susan looked up, saw the phone on the table across the room, and put her face back into her hands. She knew she wasn't seeing things. But she also knew she didn't bring the phone down from Daniel's room. And Daniel hadn't been out of bed in weeks, so it was unlikely he'd brought it down. If neither of them, then who? How? And why did everything about Daniel's illness make her stomach do rolls?

She asked these things of Peter later that night as they lay in bed, shivering. The house had somehow, over the past few days, stopped retaining heat, so while it was beautiful weather outside, inside, at night, they froze. Peter listened to her and wished he could offer something that would help, but he was just as dumbfounded by everything that was happening. That was the point at which they both finally started admitting, to themselves—neither of them said a word out loud, not even to each other—that maybe the boy in the room upstairs was less their son, and more something else.

This took a reworking of his belief system on Peter's part, but there was nothing like inexplicable proof to sway a skeptical mind.

· · · ·

PETER'D HAD THE WORST time of it. It was bad enough watching his son devolve before his eyes into something that should never have seen the sun. It was worse seeing what it was doing to his wife. Susan, who had been the one to help Daniel back to sleep when he had a nightmare, Susan who could rearrange her schedule to accommodate an early out at school, or a sick day, Susan who never once had failed to be there for Daniel. It was Susan's devotion to the boy that Peter attributed to his own laxness. She was on top of it, so he didn't have to be. And now he was watching the thing in the back room—by this time he'd stopped thinking of it as Daniel—destroy her. He had the sense at one point she was about to leave. She'd come out of the room crying, saying the thing had told her their son was dead.

If she believed that for even a second, Peter thought, he could imagine her leaving and not looking back. If Daniel was gone, she could leave everything she had and just go. What was there to stay for? Peter could go with her, of course, but with or without him, she was leaving.

He never asked her if this was her plan, but he sensed it might be.

Before she could act, though, he came home one afternoon to find her dead at the bottom of the stairs.

Now it was just Peter and the demon. Whatever affect it had had on Susan, Peter couldn't bring himself to accept that Daniel was gone for good. And if he couldn't be sure, he couldn't leave, even if it meant spending his days changing shit-covered sheets and spooning baby food into the thing's mouth, while trying to hold down what little he'd been able to eat that day.

Peter got out of bed and went downstairs. The kitchen was silent. Last week the thing had cut the power to the house. Everything in the refrigerator had spoiled, but it wouldn't let him open it to throw any of it out and the stench hung thick in the air. Everything Peter ate came from the pantry. Soups mostly, anything else the thing made rotten. Bread grew mold the second it was opened. Crackers and chips went stale. It let him live on canned soups, which he had to eat cold, while it sucked down baby food by the case, laughing at him behind Daniel's face smeared with fruit.

He hated the thing. He wished again that he could believe he'd never get Daniel back, so he'd have the freedom to beat the thing to a pulp.

He pulled open a drawer and saw a knife lying there. He pulled it out, looked at it in the light that streamed in over the sink. It was covered in Susan's blood and when Peter glanced into the other room, he saw her lying there at the bottom of the stairs, dead and bloody. Peter knelt over her with the knife in his hand.

He blinked and the vision was gone.

That wasn't how it happened at all. The thing upstairs killed her. Not with a knife, her neck was broken in the fall down the stairs. Maybe it made her trip, maybe it pushed her, but whatever it was, the thing upstairs killed her, not Peter.

He put the knife away, closed the drawer, and took a glass from the sink. He ran water into it, gulped it down before tasting the rust and dirt in it.

He spit it out and said, "Shit!"

He forgot the thing had clogged the pipes. He tossed the glass into the sink and it shattered.

Peter returned to bed and lay awake staring into the dark. He didn't know how long it was, but he heard something downstairs. His first thought was, It's trying to get out. It had finally managed to get Daniel out of bed and down the stairs and now it wanted to do to the world what it had done to Peter and Susan.

He wanted to stay in bed, to let it go, to let it be someone else's problem. But it was still his son and that meant it was his responsibility. It was up to him to stop it.

He went downstairs and approached the door, but saw no one there. The knock came again and Peter moved closer. Maybe it had come out of Daniel and was just the spirit that wanted out now, maybe that's why he couldn't see it.

But when the knock came again, followed by a voice, "Peter. You in there?" he realized it wasn't anything trying to get out, but someone outside, wanting in.

Why would anyone want to come into this place?

Because they don't know, he remembered. He couldn't risk exposing anyone else to this.

"Who is it?" he asked.

"Pete? That you? It's Mark, come on, let me in."

"Mark? It's the middle of the night."

"It's eleven thirty, Pete."

That early? What time had he gone to bed?

"It's not a good time." He paused, his head almost resting against the door, knowing freedom lay on the other side, knowing he could never taste it again. "Daniel's sleeping. He doesn't feel well. I'll give you a call in the morning."

"What?" the voice on the other side asked. "Daniel? Peter, come on, man, you have to let me in. We have to talk."

"Not tonight, Mark. I'll call you in the morning."

"Did you say Daniel's sick?"

"Yeah, I think he's got food poisoning or something. He's sleeping, though, so just go on home and we'll talk later."

Peter waited for Mark to go away. How long since he'd heard from him? At least since Susan's funeral. That was the last time Peter'd heard from anyone, the last time he'd gone to work, the last time he'd done anything. He was allowed to shop at the all-night convenient store down the block, but only for thirty minutes. Anything longer and the demon made Peter's head ring until he was practically running back to the house and darting inside. One more way it would keep him in its service forever.

"Peter?" Mark asked from outside.

Peter waited.

"Peter, Daniel died over a month ago. A couple weeks before Susan left. You gotta let me in, man. Come on, I haven't seen you in weeks. Susan called me. She said you might need someone to look in on you. Said you weren't taking any of this too well."

Peter had heard the first part, but everything after "let me in" was drowned out by the ringing in Peter's head. The demon knew what was happening and wanted it stopped. He had to move away from the door to make the ringing calm down, but until Mark was gone it wouldn't stop completely.

"I have to go," Peter called. "Daniel's calling for me. I'll call you tomorrow, Mark."

He ran upstairs and closed himself in his room.

The ringing faded to a quiet hum, just low enough to let him hear Mark pounding on the front door again.

Why would Mark say something like that?

Daniel was sick months ago, yes, but that had only been the beginning of what Peter now knew had been the truth. There was no disease in Daniel but the demon, and while he now doubted whether or not heaven and hell were real, he knew the angels and devils existed, and they lived on earth inside any of us they chose.

Mark was still pounding on the door, but over that Peter heard the beast calling for him.

He got out of bed and walked down the hall, fearful at seeing Daniel again and noticing some new deformity the demon had wrought on him. Already the boy's body was shriveling, curling in on itself, his skin turning to scales, his face long and hollow. Peter wondered how much longer before the horns broke through the skin on Daniel's head. He'd seen them forming for a couple days.

He stopped outside the door and thought again of Mark's comment.

Daniel died over a month ago. A couple weeks before Susan left.

If that were true, he reasoned, he would open this door and Daniel would be gone. If Daniel were gone, he couldn't be here, it was simple as that.

If Daniel were gone, Peter would be free and his nightmare over and the demon exposed as a figment of his guilty imagination. He would seek help, but in time he would be fine.

He opened the door.

"I'm hungry," the demon croaked. "Please feed me, daddy."

It laughed.

Heaven or hell, he couldn't say, but he knew where the demons lived. He closed the door and went down to get a jar of baby food. He thought if he could just hold on a little longer, the thing would get what it came for and leave Peter and Daniel in peace.

Prompt #5:

Pick a favorite book and write a follow-up, whether a full sequel (make sure it's in the public domain), or just a short story about what happened next. While STRANGE CASE OF DR. JEKYLL AND MR. HYDE isn't my favorite novel, I did feel inspired after reading it, and I came up with this story:

THE DICHOTOMY OF MONSTERS

. . . .

CONSCIOUSNESS CAME in like a merry-go-round, spinning up from somewhere deep below until he was aware of his eyes rolling behind his closed lids, of his chest expanding with each breath, and a distinct feeling of moss growing inside his mouth.

He kept still and listened to make sure he was alone. If they saw him moving now, everything would be ruined. He heard movement and voices outside, possibly coming from upstairs, but definitely not in the room, nor even just outside it. He flexed his fingers and toes, moved his arms and sat up. His eyes focused with a weariness that told of the toll his efforts had taken the past year. They glowed red with exhaustion and he wanted nothing more than to close them again and sleep the night through. Well, almost nothing more. The mission was still at hand.

Hyde got to his feet, slowly and with a hand on the edge of the desk for balance. The door had been broken in, so he knew they had seen him. Who? Probably only the butler, and that lawyer. They would have to die, of course; his body couldn't suddenly come up missing. If the numbers hadn't been in their favor, he would have killed whoever came through that door. But two of them, (at least, and who knew how many more in the house would have come running when they heard the commotion) were half too many, and the first thing to come to his mind had been the drug, which paralyzed him for several hours, giving the appearance of death. He knew only his death would put them at ease, and then he could much more easily catch them off guard.

The butler, Poole, was first. Hyde strangled him while the old man sat at the table, holding his head in his hands and muttering over and over, "It's over now, the nightmare is over. It's over now."

"Indeed," Hyde grunted, then clamped his monstrous hands around the domestic's neck so tight Poole's eyes bulged. He thrashed, but never fought back. As if he could against his killer's brute strength. And he'd been getting stronger, hadn't he?

For good measure, he broke the footman Bradshaw's neck, then gathered the trunks he'd hidden earlier, loaded them onto the coach, and rode through the midnight streets to Utterson's house.

The lawyer was not in his house, but Hyde found him at the office. A letter lay open on the table in front of him and the lawyer looked as if he'd seen the devil himself.

Without warning, Hyde burst in, attacked the lawyer, who stared in shock at the supposedly risen corpse and shrieked, "Devil!" as the assailant beat him down with his fists, pummeling until the lawyer was a broken mass on the floor. He breathed as if his lung had collapsed, and his face was swollen to twice its size already. One arm lay broken and bent where no joint had been.

Hyde stood over him, then crouched down to look him over closer. He grunted at his victim. Utterson looked up with the one eye that hadn't filled with blood, tried to draw a breath. He croaked his killer's name, and Hyde grinned wide and wicked, then brought up his clasped fists and drove them down into Utterson's face a final time.

He looked around briefly, saw the papers on Utterson's table, and shoved them into his pocket for later review, then dashed outside to the waiting coach. He rode full speed for the dock where he'd booked passage on a ship to America, months ago, without the doctor's knowledge. He had, in fact, done many things of late without the Good Doctor's knowledge. Which worked to his advantage; if the doctor knew what Hyde knew, it could have spelled his own end instead of the other way around. As it was, Hyde was stronger than ever, and even that tickle at the back of his head he'd always considered the doctor's presence was gone.

The night had been moving forward, ever forward, and there was no time to stop now. He made the dock, had his things taken aboard, and found his cabin where he closed and locked the door. He checked his watch; the ship left port in fifteen minutes. There was no guarantee he wouldn't be found, none until the ship was out to sea and London left far behind. He stood in his room, silent, still, just waiting, listening for any sounds outside that might spell his doom. But the minutes ticked by and before he knew it, the ship was moving.

Finally, Hyde settled back into his bunk for some much needed rest, but when he turned over, he felt the ruffle of paper from Utterson's desk in his jacket pocket. He pulled out the sheets and opened them, then began to read. It was a good thing he'd thought to take it. The Good Doctor's confession would never be believed by those outside of the events, but it couldn't very well just be left lying around, either.

They deserved what they got, every last one of them. His only regret was they were still dead, as it meant he wouldn't be able to kill them again.

• • • •

THE *S.S. City of Paris* was outfitted for one thousand, seven hundred forty passengers. With a full compliment, the man in the filthy sweater would have counted as one thousand, seven hundred forty-one.

The man ducked down corridors and into a utility room where he maneuvered under and around pipes and valves, making his way through the storage compartments, and back to the deck of the ship where the chase started again. He just needed to disappear somewhere as far from his bed as he could, so that when they started searching the ship for him, they would be looking at the opposite end. But no matter how he tried to outrun or trick the cook, every time he glanced back, there the man was.

The man in the filthy sweater clutched his dinner to his chest and barreled down the hallway, almost tripping over his own feet. He flew down a flight of stairs and around a corner where he ran headfirst into an immovable object, thudded against it, and fell to the floor.

He lay sprawled there, looking up at this black figure that blocked his path, and while he couldn't place what it was, there was something his eye told him was off about it. He tried to gather his goods and take off again but the cook was close behind, and the object still blocked his path. He tried to get to his feet, even if he didn't have everything in hand, but before he could move around the man in front of him, a hand fell on his shoulder and the man in the filthy sweater gasped and tried to pull away.

The cook's grip was strong, and as he started to haul the man away, he said to Hyde, who still hadn't moved or spoken, "Thanks for catching this one for me. The Captain'll be happy to deal with him now."

The man in the filthy sweater looked up at Hyde, as if pleading for help, but the cook was yanking him along, back toward the stairs.

"I didn't do nothing," the man asserted. "A body's got to eat, doesn't he?"

"Not when you stowaway, you don't," the cook complained. "You'll be taking food out of decent paying customers' mouths."

"There's plenty on board, though. I don't eat much, you won't even notice it!"

"Hey!" the figure standing by and watching grunted. The cook and the man in the filthy sweater both stopped suddenly, surprised and curious to see what this man had to offer. The man in the sweater was still trying to pin down just what about this man looked so . . . deformed. "Let him go."

"What? Now, look here," the cook said, releasing the thief and stalking back toward Hyde, "you don't seem to understand, pal. When folks come aboard and don't pay, and then start stealing food, that's food you paid for with your own money. And you want to just let this filth go? Maybe we'll let him go, then. Maybe we'll give him your room, let him eat your meals, while you sleep in the filth and eat scraps instead, would that be better suited to you?"

The cook had time only to register the hand raising, the glint of metal in the half-light coming down the stairs, then he was on the floor, being pummeled over and over as the man beating him said only, "I said let him go!" The cane rained down blow after blow and soon the cook was curled on the floor, bloodied and swollen.

Hyde gazed down at his work, then stepped over the half-conscious man and, as he mounted the stairs, said to the man in the filthy sweater, who stood watching it all, "Bring him along."

The man dragged the beaten cook up the stairs and along the corridor, hoping no one came out of their rooms and saw him, following his savior to the aft deck where the brute stopped at the rail and said, "Toss him over."

"What?"

"Don't question me, you're wasting time and when they catch you, you're finished. Now do as I said."

The man lifted the cook, who was so much deadweight, barely aware of what was happening to him, slung part of him over the rail, looked around to make sure he wasn't seen, then, just as the cook came awake a little more and realized what was happening, lifted again and pushed, dropped the beaten man over the rear of the ship and watched him fall into the water, screaming and flailing.

The man wanted to run for the shadows, but Hyde stopped him and said, "Don't move. If anyone heard the scream, they'll come. You want to be here to assure them it was just you."

"But what am I screaming for?"

Hyde backhanded him and the man went down, spit blood, and asked, "What was that for?"

Hyde turned away, watched the water, saw the cook sink for the last time and when he didn't reappear, he grabbed the man's filthy sweater and said, "Okay, he's gone. You're with me now."

He led the man to his room after letting him stop to gather his stolen food. And that's how Hyde met Lewis Carlyle, stowaway, thief, and now murderer.

• • • •

THE TRIP TO AMERICA took just over five days to complete, and in that time Lewis had assured Hyde over and over that he was his man, whatever he needed, whatever he wanted, when they got to America, Lewis could get it for him, he knew lots of people.

Hyde then assured Lewis that, when the boat landed, there was a job he had in mind for the man.

Hyde fed the man, outfitted him with clean clothes—he seemed to have let a few of the Good Doctor's things find their way in with his own—and kept him safe from the crew. Lewis in turn kept assuring his savior that whatever it was, he'd do it, no question.

By the time the boat reached dock, Hyde had already begun to think he should have let the cook brain Carlyle as it seemed the only way to quiet the man. He asked him once, "Why do you insist on this constant, annoying chatter?" to which Lewis replied he'd spent so much time alone throughout his life, he was maybe just making up for lost conversation. "Don't worry, though," Lewis assured him, "I know when to keep quiet, too. I can keep a secret like you wouldn't believe."

New York was a sight. If Hyde had thought London was crowded, it was nothing to what he saw here. He liked it, though; it gave him more confidence he could blend in, hide amongst them, get lost in the shuffle of people.

He hired a coach and gave directions to a boarding house, although he had no plans to stay even one night there. He paid for a month, then hired that same coach to take him and Lewis to a train station.

"We just got here, though. I told you," Lewis reminded him, "whatever you need in this town, I can find it."

"What I need isn't in this town," Hyde told him.

Hyde purchased one ticket, then left instructions for Lewis and told him with a glare, "Don't fail me. Remember, you would be rotting in a hole somewhere if not for me. And you aren't the only one who can find things. I'll find you, if you disobey me. I'll be back in three days. When I return, I expect your task to be completed."

"I won't let you down," Lewis promised. "Three days."

"You'd better. And one more thing." He handed Lewis a key with an address written on it and said, "Take the other trunk here. Leave it where I'll find it, but not out in the open. Lock the door." And with that, Hyde boarded the train, leaving Lewis Carlyle to the droves of the city.

• • • •

HYDE WAS, BY HIS NATURE, a solitary creature, so the quiet of his cabin was a welcome gift. The only reason he had saved Lewis in the first place was because he saw the advantages of having someone who could take care of certain aspects of his mission while Hyde was away, thereby saving much valuable time. Before all was said and done, Hyde knew Lewis Carlyle would earn his keep one way or another.

The train traveled to Chicago, where Hyde disembarked, and immediately set off for a ruined hulk of charred wood and black, broken glass. The Sunderland Brothers warehouse used to store dry goods for various businesses, mostly food stuffs. And this is where Hyde's search, which had begun in the Good Doctor's house, had led.

The building had burned down several months ago, and there was every chance in the world that nothing inside remained. But it was the best lead Hyde had been able to establish. He stepped inside the open building, the chilly nighttime air opening his lungs and the wind scraping like knives against his skin.

He stepped slowly, cautiously, his eyes ever-open for what he sought, no idea where in this burnt-out husk it may have been kept. Birds took flight from the open rafters and he heard the squeal of rats somewhere beneath the ashy mess.

The problem, as the Good Doctor discovered, with the formula that allowed for the change back and forth—the change Hyde had eventually been able to overcome—had been possible due to a supply of tainted salts the Doctor had purchased. In his despair, the Doctor gave in, resigned himself to being drowned out by the stronger Hyde. Hyde, however, had other ideas. Those salts would come in handy.

He had written to the original supplier, inquiring about the shipment and who else may have purchased from the same lot number. He was answered with the names of three other houses, which he then wrote to. Two answered back saying once they discovered the salts had been ruined, they'd disposed of their supplies. The Sunderland Brothers Supply House wrote back to Hyde with news of the fire that had consumed their warehouse just half the year gone. Everything had been burned, they said.

Hyde searched the ruins now. He was neither demanding nor greedy; he didn't need a ton of the stuff, just enough.

He found containers of powders and seasonings along a far wall, under a flight of metal stairs that had been charred by the fire, ruined by the weather. Hyde kicked a family of possums out of their nest, cleared out a mound of shredded burlap that had somehow made it through the blaze, and there, under at least three hundred pounds of what felt like baking flour but smelled like old sweat and curdled cheese, he found it. There were three bags, still sealed, with the label barely visible anymore. He moved one, testing its strength, and it felt sturdy enough, so he lifted it over his shoulder, then the other two. The one on the bottom was covered in mold, and he dropped it, then watched the salt spread out in a fan as the bag exploded on the ground.

Hyde saw one more bag now, still hidden under the collapsed top of a wooden crate, but he left it there. If this wasn't from the same shipment as the Good Doctor's original supply, it would be worthless anyway. But if it was right, if it worked, he didn't want to have more on-hand than what he felt would be necessary for his task. He certainly saw no reason to let temptation play into matters later on. After all, it only took one more change to give the Doctor the chance to end it once and for all. If Hyde had anything to say about it, that would never happen. So he left the final bag on the ground, turned around, and strode out of the burned ruins.

The train back to New York came by in a few hours, so Hyde rested at the platform until it arrived. When the engine pulled up, hissing and steaming to a halt, he carried his bags of salt aboard, took himself to his cabin, and slept most of the ride back. Provided Lewis had done as he was told, Hyde would be a busy man upon his return.

· · · ·

THE RETURN TRIP SEEMED to take less time, so when the train pulled into the station, Hyde felt as if he'd only moments ago climbed aboard. He came down the stairs, to the platform, his boots thunking across the boards with the extra weight of the bags of salt, one under each arm. He passed by the room he'd rented when he first arrived, but didn't stop. This would not be where he spent his time.

Instead he carried the salt another ten blocks to an out of the way neighborhood and found the address of a building he'd rented from an apothecary who was moving his business to Boston. Hyde had made the arrangements weeks ago and he found the place just as he'd been promised. It was clean, boarded up, and the next building over, a dressmaker's shop, was over half the block down. The door wasn't boarded like the windows, and he pulled a key from his coat pocket, then let himself in.

The air was damp and musty from disuse in this weather, but from the looks the place would suit his purposes just fine. Lewis had left his trunk in a back room, then covered it with a sheet.

Hyde checked the building over again before going any further. There was a back door, but it was locked. The few windows were covered, and the place was, aside from Hyde himself, empty.

Taking out his trunk, Hyde opened the lid, took out the top few layers of clothes, two coats and a suit, to get at the instruments underneath. Using the apothecary's table as his workspace, Hyde set up the Good Doctor's Bunsen burner, inserted the test tubes and set up the beakers, then measured out the ingredients that made up the solution. The salts, he thought. They have to work.

Hyde filled a flask with the first batch, set it behind the counter, and left the premises, locking the door behind him.

He walked back to the boarding house and knocked on the door at the top of the stairs. A tired voice called, "Who's there?" and Hyde announced himself, followed by the door swinging open and Lewis telling him, "I found one."

"Excellent," Hyde commended him, "grab your coat, we'll celebrate. Come."

He turned without waiting and back down the stairs he went, out the door to the street, and within a minute, Lewis joined him.

"Where are we going?"

"You've still got the key I gave you?"

"Yes," Lewis replied, producing the key from his jacket pocket. Hyde took it, slipped it into his own pocket, and said, "You won't be needing it."

He led Lewis back to the shop. Inside Lewis looked around, eager to do whatever was asked of him, unsure of just what was going on.

He asked, "What's with this place, anyway? What was in the trunk?"

"We are going into business, Mr. Carlyle. I may not have told you on the ship, but I am a medical doctor, and this will be my new practice. But to do it, I'm going to need a man who knows this city and knows where to find things. Also, word of mouth. You know the people here. We'll need patients, but patients don't just appear. Spread the word, my good man."

The monologue had been practiced on the train and Hyde let it roll off his tongue.

"A toast," he said, bringing out the flask. He unscrewed the lid and handed it over, saying, "To the start of a better life in a new world."

"I'll drink to that," Lewis agreed, smiling and bringing the flask to his lips. He tossed it back, swallowed a mouthful, and asked, "So what was with needing me to find that—" and here his throat closed up and his breath shot from his body, doubling him over, taking him to his knees, gasping and convulsing.

Hyde stood aside in wonder, first hopeful, then elated as the creature that stood up in the spot where, moments ago, Lewis Carlyle had been about to ask a question, coughed out a wad of phlegm, spit into the corner, then looked up at Hyde asking, "What did you do to me?"

"I set you free," Hyde said.

$$\cdot\ \cdot\ \cdot\ \cdot$$

THE LONG DAY WAS OVER, and Bea swept up the last of the day's work, dumped it in the bin, doused the lights, and locked the door behind her as she turned up the street for home. It was late, but not so late the streets were deserted—as if they ever were in this city—but still the clop clop clop of her feet up the sidewalks seemed to echo with a certain eerie quality that made her think of fog on a chilly day, empty, open canyons, the barren alleys between the buildings after a heavy rainfall, or the open mouths of children with terror in their eyes.

She sighed, sniffed late night air, and crossed the street to avoid passing the couple sitting on a stoop just up the block. She ran through the list of things she still had to do when she got home tonight, ran through the set-up routine when she went into the shop in the morning, wishing one of these days to sleep longer than six hours. It was a sad day, she reflected, when the thought of throwing yourself down a flight of stairs in hopes of breaking a leg, a wrist, something minor but incapacitating was the better of two evils when it meant she couldn't work for a few weeks.

She didn't hear the rapidly approaching footsteps, speeding faster and faster up the sidewalk behind her, until the last second when she whirled to see what it was. The clouds parted over the moon just at the right time, giving her a look at the huge swollen eyes, both huge pits of black spite bearing down on her. The moon reflected off a protruding brow, and a hideously crooked mouth opened in glee.

· · · ·

"YOU BROUGHT ME A BAKER?" Hyde said. The contempt dripped from his mouth like drool. "I left you with very specific instructions, Mr. Carlyle, and this is what you bring to me? A baker! What am I supposed to do with her?"

"I know what you said, Mr. Hyde. And I did as you asked. She works in the bakery. But, remember, friend, you're not from here. You don't know this one. It was in all the papers, what she did. Even if they never found their proof."

This got the man's attention.

"Do tell, Mr. Carlyle."

"She's a murderess, Mr. Hyde. What you see before you is a lonely woman who works in a baker's shop to make her money because no one wanted her on the streets; they were all afraid. She used to be Mrs. Douglas White. Wife of a very distinguished lawyer in this city. She bore his children, kept his house. Then one day, the man comes home, goes inside, finds his poor children dead, the wife unconscious. So the story goes as she tells it. Whoever came in and did the children in then took care of the husband as well. When the missus woke up, she was a childless widow. Truth is, however, Mr. Hyde, she killed the lot of them."

"And how are you so sure of this?"

"Everyone knows it. The husband had been checking up on his beautiful wife, see. He fathered no children, yet they had two in the home. She was about to be a divorcee, out on the streets with two children to raise on her own. There are no secrets in these neighborhoods."

"You'd better hope for your sake, Mr. Carlyle, that you are wrong about that."

"Don't need hope when I can come and go as someone else, eh? I like this, by the way. I think—"

"It won't last," Hyde interrupted, studying the unconscious woman before him.

"What?"

"You'll be back to regular Lewis Carlyle soon enough."

"But, I don't want to be normal Lewis Carlyle."

"For the foreseeable future, what you want is of no consequence."

Hyde approached the woman, leaned down and inspected her face.

"Murderess, you say?"

"Everyone knows it, they just couldn't find any proof to put her way with."

"Well," Hyde said, "we'll see when she wakes up, then we'll know how well you've done."

"She's an evil one," Lewis said, then he staggered backward, bent over, vomited, and passed out. He woke up moments later, shrunken, re-fitted, back to, as Mr. Hyde had said, "regular Lewis Carlyle."

"Go home," Hyde said. "I'll be busy here for a while."

"When can I get some more of that?"

Hyde gave Lewis a look that told the smaller man to stop asking questions and do as he was told. Which he did. He went out the back way, as Hyde instructed, so as not to attract attention. When he was gone, Mr. Hyde took the woman into the back room, bound her to a work table, then prepared the formula.

• • • •

BEA WOKE SCREAMING.

Or rather, she would have been screaming, had Hyde not gagged her. But her struggles and the muffled noises coming from her were screams enough.

"Shut it!" Hyde ordered, and when she looked up, saw this beast looking down on her, Bea did as she was told. Hyde thought she had very striking eyes when they were opened. They watched him as he crossed the room and picked up a beaker of liquid.

"Very good," he said. "My name is Hyde. You're here at my request because my associate says you possess certain traits I seek. You murdered your husband and children, yes?"

She shook her head no.

"We shouldn't start lying to each other already," Hyde admonished. "The truth. You murdered your husband and children. Yes? I'm no policeman, and since you and I are about to be very well-acquainted, we might as well be open."

She hesitated. Her eyes roamed the walls, the ceiling, every inch of the room that she could see from the table. She looked back to Hyde and whined again. She said something around the gag, but he couldn't make it out.

"Answer the question, then I take it off," he said.

She finally nodded her head.

The smile that spread across the beast's face was hideous, he knew, but he always received a small dose of enjoyment at the reactions of others upon seeing that evil grin.

"That is very good news," he said. "You might just work out. Now, I will take off the gag, but believe me when I say the first noise to escape your mouth that doesn't suit me, I will snap your neck like a twig. Do you understand?"

She nodded again.

Hyde took off the gag, and she opened her mouth to speak before he stopped her and said, "I mean it."

"What kind of beast are you?"

"I'm not a beast, dear. I'm just a man. My childhood may have differed from yours in that I didn't have one . . . Yes, I sprang whole from the womb to live and do as I may without care for consequence. So according to what I've heard about you, by your own admission, we're not so different after all."

Bea looked around the room, then at the straps holding her down.

"What do you want with me? I haven't any money. You can do to me what you will, but if you're after ransom, you've wasted your time."

"I'm not after your money. I have something for you."

And before she could reply, Hyde pulled the syringe from his coat pocket, jabbed it into her neck, and pressed the plunger.

He pulled the needle from her, then stepped back.

The Good Doctor always drank the formula, but Hyde assumed this would work just as well. She opened her mouth to scream at the heat tearing through her—Hyde knew it well—and that's when he realized he should have left the gag in place. He slapped his hand over her mouth, trying to quiet her while her body struggled against the bindings that held her down. The shift came on like a steam engine, and her whole body went into a state of shock as every cell in it was turned inside out, broken down, reformed and rearranged. While normally an average-looking woman, Bea's features now revealed the true ugliness inside her. Hyde kept her quiet while the change worked its way through her. She struggled, she whipped her head from side to side trying to loose the shriek that issued unending from her throat. Her mouth worked as she tried to bite Hyde's fingers off. He worked the gag back into her mouth, and then her struggles ceased and all was quiet. Hyde stepped away to admire what he'd done.

He couldn't help but smile, even though he knew his work wasn't yet near done with her. It would take many more injections, who knew how much time before the change was involuntary, and then permanent. His own evolution took years, but then the Good Doctor had taken months between changes. Hyde didn't have years. He'd be lucky, he knew, if he had even one. He had to work fast.

He looked at the woman. The suddenness of the change, caused by the injection, had sent her into shock and she stared at him now, unmoving, unresponsive. That was the effect he had hoped for, and if he had his way, this would be the state she would remain in during their time together.

• • • •

HYDE STAYED IN THE empty shop with the woman, holed up day and night. Lewis brought him food and supplies, like a cot Hyde set up next to his betrothed. He didn't sleep much, but he did sleep, and it was always light, and plagued with fleeting dreams of death.

Bea made it through a change with her senses intact on the eighth day. It was beginning to take longer for her to revert back, and on this particular day, after the change took place, as Hyde was across the room mixing the next injection, she came out of her shock ten minutes in.

"I know what you want," she croaked, and the sudden voice in the silence gave Hyde a thrill.

"You're awake?"

"All the same. I know what you want, villain. Are you so pathetic you have to take it like this?"

"Hmm," Hyde pondered. "What is it you think I want?"

"It's obvious. You're a man. You want what every man wants. It's all they've ever wanted from me. But don't think you'll find me such easy prey."

"You're already on my table," he pointed out.

"But I bite back," she warned him. "I'll get out of here, and I'll bash your brains in with a frying pan. I'll skewer your eyes with a fireplace poker. I'll toss you into the alley and let the rats eat away your—"

"I wouldn't count on any of that," Hyde said. "You're not the only murderer in this room."

She stared at him. He mixed the final ingredients, readied the next syringe, then set it aside.

Then he pulled a stool near the table, took a seat, and leaned in to examine her.

"You are quite a creature," he said. "Not much to look at, I admit, but I do like your will. I think you might be the one to carry it to term."

"What?"

"Woman, I don't give two pence for your body. If that's all I were interested in, I've had more than you, I've had better than you. Some gave willingly, but not all. That never stopped me. If that's all I wanted, I'd have discarded your broken body days ago."

"Carry what to term?" she asked.

"My son," he replied. The horror on her face made Hyde laugh out loud. She looked down at her body, and Hyde said, "No, no, I haven't done anything yet. I want to wait with you, I want to make sure your changes are done. The union must be pure. That was always the problem with the ones who came before you, see. I tried to unite my superior, stronger genetic material with the weaker, less adept women back home. Unfortunately, none of them made it. Only two even took, and they both died a week into conception. Obviously I needed something, someone, stronger, someone like me, who could bear the weight, the burden, of my child."

"You wouldn't."

"I will, and you should be glad for it, because it's the only thing keeping you alive. Is it ego, or just a being's natural survival instinct that drives it to procreation? The Good Doctor tried to have me done with, you know. Tried to erase me from the face of the earth, to scour the stain of my existence from history. But you and I are going to make sure that doesn't happen. The Good Doctor's legacy lives on in me, and mine will live on through you once I'm gone. I will neither be forgotten nor denied, no matter how much it means I have to put you through."

She looked at him and for the first time he saw real fear in her. He enjoyed it. This would be a very promising union.

* * * *

THE FIRST AUTOMATIC change came a week later.

Lewis had brought Hyde's dinner and afterward the two shared a drink. Lewis was playing with a gun he'd stolen from a house he'd burgled, trying to impress Hyde with his prowess, but Hyde was barely paying attention. His eyes were on the woman.

They'd been isolated in this back room for two weeks now, she'd never left the table, even to relieve herself. Hyde fed and tended to her, all the while she lay strapped in, waiting for this moment. She made a noise in her sleep, and Hyde watched, fascinated again, and now elated as well, to see her form—her new true form—boiling just below the surface. Her skin toughened and her muscles gained mass and density. Admittedly not a beautiful woman, her features darkened further, giving her a, not necessarily stupid appearance, but definitely more brutal.

Considering her background, Hyde knew her alternate form wouldn't be weak as he had been in the beginning, when the Good Doctor was just then beginning to explore his darker side. This woman had been exploring her darker side for some time, so when her change happened, her other form was bigger, stronger, more assertive. She would never slink among the shadows or flee an altercation as Hyde had done in the past. He could never allow her to escape this room, he knew that, even if it meant tending to her the entire nine months of her gestation. He was, by no means, afraid of her, but someone like this, someone who had spent so much of her life already embracing that side of themselves, there was no predicting the lengths she would go to for revenge—and he never doubted for an instant revenge would be the only thing on her mind.

He had to smile and when he did, Lewis glanced over to see what had made such a repulsive look come across this man's face. Lewis gasped and asked, "Is she doing that on her own? You didn't even inject her."

"That was the point of all this," Hyde said. "It won't be long now."

"What's going to happen?"

"I'm going to keep injecting her. It's even more important now that she maintain this form. Now that she's doing it on her own, it's going to keep happening, but the frequency will fluctuate unless I keep her like this. Note the time, Mr. Carlyle; I want to track how long she stays like this on her own. I'm going to prepare an injection, so when she does revert back, I can put her back again."

"It's just going on eleven o'clock," Lewis announced, then closed his pocket watch and put it away again.

Hyde was at the workspace, measuring, pouring, mixing, then drawing up the contents into the syringe. Meanwhile Lewis moved closer to Bea who was beginning to wake up. Her blurry eyes looked around, taking in the scene. She saw Lewis and said, "You know what he wants to do to me? Did he tell you?"

Lewis shook his head.

"He wants to make babies with me. Isn't that a riot? A beast like him, and a woman like me."

Lewis listened, transfixed. Hyde set his syringe on a tray and came over.

"That's exactly what I plan to do," he said. "And now that you're changing involuntarily, it won't be long."

She chuckled, then turned to Lewis again and said, "He thinks I'm like him. Rotten to the core."

"Is that a fact?" Lewis asked. He was nodding along.

"Who wouldn't think it, after what you told him I did?"

"I admit," Hyde said, "I had my reservations at first. A baker, of all things. But after seeing you like this, I am very very pleased with Mr. Carlyle's choice."

"You didn't tell him everything, obviously," she said to the quiet Mr. Carlyle.

"No, I guess I didn't." He backed away, sank into the room, away from the table.

"Is that so?" Hyde asked. He turned to Lewis. "What more is there?"

"He didn't tell you about the other," the woman said. "I killed my husband and my children, yes. But he only told you the stories that had made the rounds of the neighborhood."

"What he told me was enough," Hyde said.

"But it wasn't," Bea replied. "What the gossips didn't know about is the other one I killed, the last one."

Hyde looked to Carlyle. The man shrugged and took another step back.

"Do tell," Hyde said.

"The baby in my womb that no one knew about. No one but me. I did a horrible job of it, though. Tore myself up something awful. I promise one thing: there's never a chance in the world I'll have another child. Not because I choose—although I definitely choose not to—but because I just don't have it in me anymore. To save me, the surgeons had to remove the whole works."

Hyde looked back again at Carlyle, but the man was looking at the floor.

"You can try all you like," she laughed, "you'll never have a child from me."

"Did you know about this?" Hyde asked. Then he heard a CLICK near his ear, and he turned to see the barrel of Carlyle's stolen gun aimed at his head.

"What's this?" The rage blossomed in Hyde's face like a boiler about to explode.

"I don't want any trouble, sir," Carlyle replied. "I really don't. And I'm grateful for the way you saved me on that ship, and for this opportunity you've given us, but it's gone on long enough. A good confidence man knows when to make his exit."

"Us?" Hyde asked.

"When you showed me what that potion can do, we knew it was our ticket. It took some convincing on my part, but when she saw what it did for me . . ." He looked at her. "How could she say no? I think I've seen you mix it up enough to know how it goes, but—"

"But if it's going to start happening on its own," Bea interjected, "and then all the time, well—"

"That kind of makes the power moot, now, dunnit?"

"Now, if you'd be so kind as get me off this God forsaken table!?"

"Sorry, love. Right away," he said.

Carlyle handed her the gun and she kept it trained on Hyde while Lewis unbound her. He helped her stand, which didn't go so well and she stumbled at first on shaky legs. She cracked her knees on the hard floor and Hyde backed up, hoping to escape. But the gun came up again quick and she said, "You stay put right there. I'm fine."

Hyde stopped.

Carlyle went around to the workspace.

"How long do you think before it wears off on its own?" he asked Hyde.

"An hour maybe," he said. "I can't say; I only have my own experience to go by, and mine usually came during sleep, like this one. I don't know how long they lasted."

"Well," Carlyle said. "Since we don't want her like this more than necessary, I think we'll let her change back on her own and just let it be at that until we have need of the change again."

"I promise you," Hyde said, his eyes locked on the woman and the gun, but his words clearly meant for his betrayer, "you will live to regret this."

"Half right," Carlyle replied. "I'll live, at least. Don't see regretting it, but I'm pretty sure we won't be needing this just yet. Here, you have it." And with that he stabbed the syringe into Hyde's neck, flooded the monster's veins with the potion, and immediately Hyde went to his knees as a fire filled every inner inch.

"What did you do?" he shrieked, clutching his neck where the needle had entered. He convulsed and broke out in a sweat.

Bea moved back, but didn't turn away. She watched fascinated and repulsed.

Lewis Carlyle kept one eye on the proceedings as the other focused on the equipment and ingredients, piling everything into the trunk from which Hyde had pulled it out only a few weeks ago.

Hyde himself was on the floor, struggling for balance, trying to fight through the burning in his blood. He tried to crawl toward the woman, reaching out for her, perhaps for the gun. She moved back to the wall and aimed at him, saying, "Stop moving, or I will shoot you in the head."

Hyde didn't care, the agony he was going through after so long—not just physically, but the plans he'd laid so carefully were all undone in one moment—made him hope for death. He would end this whole farce if he could just reach that pistol!

Carlyle sealed up the trunk and looked up to say, "Just shoot him and let's get out of here."

"We wanted to get out of here without attracting attention."

"Oh for God's sake," Lewis sighed. He picked up Hyde's cane from its resting place against the wall and strode to the still-writhing beast on the floor. Hyde was considerably smaller now, and looked almost handsome, although the sneer across his face when he spied Lewis was even uglier than Hyde's normal face.

"You murdered your entirely family in cold blood and you can't shoot one dying beast when he's already on the floor."

He swung into Hyde's skull with all the power in his limbs, spit flying from his mouth. He did it again, then again.

Hyde went down, but a twitch of his arms made Carlyle go for one more blow, which was the chance Hyde needed to grab the cane, yank it from his attacker's grasp, and use it to bring the man to the floor.

He was up in a flash, smaller, more nimble, faster.

Bea still hesitated, but when Jekyll reached for something to hurl at her, the bedpan Hyde had been using for her, she fired anyway, and the explosion as Jekyll's throat was torn open sounded with a flash and the sickening stench of burnt flesh, then the air was filled with the tang of blood.

Jekyll fell over, holding a hand to each side of his neck, choking on his blood.

Lewis staggered to his feet, then to the trunk.

"Let's go," he said. "Before anyone comes."

He grabbed the trunk, then saw the bag of salt under the counter. He'd forgot to pack it. No time to fumble with the locks. He grabbed the sack and hauled it off the floor, but Jekyll lashed out with the cane, the metal tip of which snagged the sack, tearing it open. Salt went everywhere.

"Come on," Bea said. But before she could make it to the door, she too was on her knees.

"Not now!" Lewis yelled. "There's no time."

But it couldn't be helped. Her change had come to an end and she reverted to her original form. Her stomach heaved and her lungs fought to draw in some of the breath expelled as they shrank to their original size.

She fought to get through it as quickly as possible.

Lewis said, "I know it hurts, but it's going to be something when we can do whatever we want like that, then go about our day like normal. You know that, right?"

"Yes," she said, managing to get to her feet again. "It's going to be worth it. You got everything?"

"In the trunk."

"That?" she asked, motioning to the pile of spilled salt.

"Salt," he replied. "We can get salt anywhere. We have to get away from here."

They ran into their future, leaving behind, or so they believed, their regrets and sins, and into a better, brighter tomorrow.

Jekyll bled out at the neck and the blood wound around the imperfections in the floor, mingling with the spilled salt, which glistened in the light.

Pick a person you see every day, and write a story about them. For me, I had a manager in the fast food place I used to work, and this manager only had one leg. We all knew he had a prosthetic leg, but no one was sure which was which, and no one wanted to ask. So I answered the question myself in a story.

Other stories written using this prompt are:

1. "fruit, unpunctured..."
2. The Stand-In
3. Safe at Home

BOB'S LEG

(originally published in Dark Matter, 2000 edition*)*

• • • •

ALTHOUGH EVERYONE WAS curious, no one wanted to ask. Jared was no different.

"Just make it sound casual," Steven said.

"Yeah," Jared scoffed. "I can do that. Hey Bob, how much did we do that hour? By the way, how'd you lose the leg, and while we're on the subject, which leg is it that's prosthetic? Would you like me to check drive-thru's trash before you fire me? Yeah, real casual."

"Come on," Steven urged. "It's not like we don't know he's only got one leg. It's not like the fact is going to be any surprise to him. What, he woke up one morning and, look, one of his legs is gone. He's got to be used to people asking by now."

"Fine," Jared said. "Then you ask."

"Shit, no!"

Then the conversation ceased as Bob came around the corner. He opened one of the cash drawers and began counting out the money. "Hey, Steven," he said, "would you sweep front line before you go? Thanks." Steven quickly grabbed a broom and began sweeping the front line of the fast food restaurant they all worked in while Jared disappeared around the corner and began running hot water into a mop bucket and the mop sink.

The restaurant was empty at this time of the afternoon and the front line was almost totally silent, save the swishing of the broom, the splatter of the mop water, the tapping of Bob's change as he counted it out on the counter, and a quiet, breathy whistle coming from Bob's pursed lips.

Steven reached the drive-thru area where he could see Jared. Jared noticed him and looked up to see Steven mouthing, "Ask him. Come on. Ask."

"You," Jared mouthed back.

"Fuck that," Steven's lips formed. He stopped sweeping and, not seeing a dust pan on front line, went to get the one by Jared.

"Come on, do you wanna know which one it is, or not? You know you do. Just ask him. Now's the perfect time. He's having a good day, he's in a good mood. Shit, he's whistling *Chattahoochee*. Just ask."

Jared dumped in a packet of floor cleaner, crumpled the empty pack and tossed it away.

"Fine," he said, annoyed with Steven's insistence. What difference did it make? Regardless of whether or not they knew which leg Bob was missing, he'd still be missing it, so nothing would be gained by the knowledge other than that uneasy awareness you get when there's something you shouldn't know about someone, but you know it anyway. But Steven wasn't going to let up, so at least Jared would have Steven off his back.

"Hey, Bob," Jared said as if the thought had occurred just then. "Out of curiosity, which leg is it you're missing? Just out of curiosity, nothing personal."

Bob stopped counting in the middle of the pennies and simply swept the rest of them into their tray, his face losing all trace of good mood. He seemed to be considering whether to answer or walk away. He made his choice and spoke to Jared without looking at him.

"What difference does it make?"

"None, really. Like I said, just out of curiosity."

"Curiosity, huh?" Bob's gaze seemed focused on the miniature Statue of Liberty in the park across the street. He had an air of distraction, as if his mind weren't totally on Jared's query, or even on this plane of existence. Finally he spoke again, only to repeat himself. "Curiosity."

"Mm-hmm. I mean, if you'd rather not," Jared said all understanding in his voice, "that's okay. It's no big deal—."

"If it were no big deal, you wouldn't have asked."

"I told you," Jared said, "it's no big deal. You don't have to answer. Just forget it, okay?"

Steven was sweeping his floor trash into a dust pan, taking his time so as not to miss any of the exchange.

"I'd forget it if I could, Jared. Trust me." There was a moment of silence. Then Bob said, "I'll show you. Then I'll tell you how I lost it. Come on."

Without waiting for Jared, Bob took off for the bathroom. Jared followed and soon the bathroom door was closed, locked, and Bob was lifting his uniform's pant leg.

"Good thing nobody sees us like this," Jared tried to joke.

Bob was silent, his face an exercise in seriousness. He pulled the cuff up to his fake knee and stared straight ahead into Jared's eyes.

Jared glanced down and saw Bob's prosthetic left leg. Well, he thought, no wonder no one could tell. That looks just like a real leg, except it's rubber.

"Happy now?" Bob uttered deadpan.

"Totally," Jared said, and began to go for the door.

"No," Bob said. "I haven't told you how I lost it."

Silence. Then:

"Well? How'd you lose it?"

"The other leg," Bob answered.

"Huh?"

"The other leg. Never go to Enlil," Bob said and dropped his pant leg. Then he grabbed the right cuff and hiked it up to above his knee.

Jared looked down and saw at least two dozen thin, pink scars covering Bob's real leg from the knee down. Then the scars stretched, spread, yawned open, becoming two dozen sneering tiny mouths. The mouths smiled and each contained double rows of pointed teeth and long, forked tongues. Jared gasped. Half of the mouths opened wide and spit tiny, splinter-like objects into Jared's body, paralyzing him.

"The other leg ate it," Bob said. "Like I said, never go to Enlil. It's a magic place, a bad place. This leg ate the other one. Sometimes it does get hungry. Like now." And he took a prosthetic step toward Jared, raising the other, monster leg.

Steven stood at the front of the counter wondering what was taking so long. Finally, the door opened, just a few inches. Bob peeked around and said, "Steven, you might as well see too. I know you're dying to."

Steven smiled and went to the bathroom to see for himself which of Bob's legs was fake and why.

Write a story using only 100 words.

This is a great exercise and can result in some very interesting tales. Other stories I've written using this prompt are:

1. Winter's Reign
2. The Laughing Picture
3. High!
4. Patches

GHOSTWRITING

(originally published online in Flash Fantastic*)*

. . . .

IN HIS WILL, LESTER left a novel and royalties to Peter. All Peter had to do was finish it. The problem was five years of writer's block.

Still, Peter tried. Weeks rolled into months as the screen stared back, unmarred.

Then, slowly, words came. His joy soared as his craft returned, words flowing like wine from his fingers, the clacking of keys like the voices of angels.

At *The End*, Peter looked over the pages, pleasure becoming confusion as he saw Lester's writing, not his. Peter screamed when the mirror showed Lester grinning back, emerging a page at a time.

Write a story using a mythical figure of fantasy, like Santa Claus, the Easter Bunny, the Tooth Fairy, as the antagonist.

The following story is a combination of two prompts, actually. I had the title "Working for the Fat Man" from a song by The Escape Club for a while, but there were several directions I could have taken. Then I saw an anthology seeking submissions for Christmas-themed stories, and I knew this was the direction this story needed to go:

WORKING FOR THE FAT MAN

(originally published in Terrible Thrills*)*

· · · ·

WORKING FOR THE FAT Man has never been easy. It used to be fun, but never easy. The hours are long, the work is demanding, and when the busy season hits, forget about it. The only reprieve is the one day a year he takes off. But when he gets back, it's the same crap all over again.

"Jolly old elf" my ass. That fat bastard hasn't been jolly in a good long time. Ever since the toy manufacturers started turning out the toys kids really want. Who needs one of his wooden trains or a colorful top, when they can have a water gun bigger than they are that shoots a spray over seventy feet? Now *that's* a fun toy. I assume. He won't let us play with that stuff. Every toy you could ever imagine, he's got it. He calls it his "market research." You'd think he'd let us see the stuff. After all, we're the ones making the toys.

Plus he won't let us compete with the big boys. When the toys started changing, we had to keep recycling the same tired old crap. How does he expect us to improve in our craft if we're not allowed to try new things?

You know, we understand that it's because of him we're still around, we know he saved us. We know that, in the real world down there, we never would have made it. So we owe him for that. But we're artists, professionals, craftsmen. And for the past hundred years, give or take, he's just become a bitter old man.

Working for the Fat Man ain't what it used to be.

It's even worse now. But that's my fault.

· · · ·

HE ALWAYS TAKES ONE of us with him on his runs. Ten years ago, I got to go along. The ride was fun, I'd never been that high, nor flown that fast before. I can see why he sticks with the sleigh instead of something more conventional. And the possibility of tumbling over the side and falling to your death makes it even more exhilarating. You hang on for dear life, and when he snaps those reigns and they take off, you know death is only a sweaty palm and a lost grip away. You get going fast enough, the wind rushing past drowns out even the loudest scream.

People think he stops time when he goes out. He just slows it down. He doesn't have to stop it. Think about it, when it's December 24th in one part of the world, it's still only December 23rd in another part, so he doesn't have to stop time. As long as he keeps up with the nightfall, it's Christmas Eve for twenty-four hours *somewhere* in the world. There's a lot of backtracking and moving up and down the latitude lines, but for someone who can move between the ticks of a second and can get into even the most secure home, the trip isn't that difficult to make.

Now if only he could figure out a way to make the work less tiring. For us, time was still moving, so by the time we'd reached North America, it seemed we'd been at it for weeks. For everyone else, it was still the middle of the night on Christmas Eve, but I was exhausted.

He came to a stop on top of an old apartment building and before I could get the bag down off the back, he grabbed my shoulder and said, "Here, I got something else for you this time."

He reached into his coat and pulled out his List. He unrolled it, and handed it to me.

"Third one down on the right," he said. "Get him."

I looked at the list, watched the names appear, move around, settle into position. The third one down on the right was Stephen Akins. The name opposite his, on the left side of the paper—the Good side—was Sean Akins. They were twins. That's how he usually does it, he never takes an only child. Take one of two or more and everything . . . well, I'm getting to it, just a second.

So while he was leaving his gifts, I got into the Akins house and into the boys' room. Down the hall, I took note of a picture on the wall, the boys together against a fake background. Like most twins, they shared a room. I went over to Stephen's bed and watched him. *How did you know which was which?* is the question, isn't it? I just did. The same way he leaves gifts for every child but no one ever wonders where it came from. Things just happen for the Fat Man and anyone who works for him. I knew as soon as I stepped into the room which was which.

But I stepped away from Stephen's bed and knelt instead in front of Sean.

"Wake up, Sean." The boy—he had to be ten—worked open one eye, saw me, and sat up.

His shock came at someone being in his room, not at *my* being there. At ten, there's still some magic in the world.

"Christmas," he said.

"That's right," I answered. "Everything you've ever been told is true, Sean. And look at this." I showed him the list and pointed to his name in the left-hand column. "This is the list of good boys and girls," I said. "Your name's on here. And guess what that means."

He shrugged. "I get everything I wanted this year?"

"Oh you get more than that," I told him. "You get to visit Santa in his workshop. Every year he picks one special boy or girl and they get to come back with him for a visit. You'll be there and back before morning, and when you wake up, everything you wanted all year will be under the tree waiting for you."

He leapt up and went for the door.

"Let's go!"

"Wait," I stopped him. "Let me help you."

I waved my hand in front of him and Sean went to sleep. I'm only a little smaller than him, but strong for my size, so carrying him back to the sleigh was no problem.

Stephen never moved. On the way back down the hall, I saw that picture I'd noted earlier. But now it was a picture of just one boy. That's what I was talking about a second ago, how he takes one of the set and everything changes. I don't know who it was he made his deals with so long ago, but it must have been someone very powerful.

Back on the roof of the building, he was waiting for us.

"What took so long?"

"He tried to run and yell when he saw me in his room," I said. "He's a bad one all right."

"Good. Come on."

I hopped in, stuffed the boy into the back, and we finished the nights' deliveries.

When we returned to the shop, he unloaded the boy himself and carried him inside.

Everyone welcomed me back and we went to the shop for a drink and something to eat. Meanwhile, the Fat Man took the boy into the shop's back room. This was where he always took them. None of us had ever been in there, nor did we want to go. We hadn't been in, but we'd heard sounds coming from there, and the worst of them came when Fat Man was gone, so what else was in there besides him was anyone's guess. We were happy to let it stay that way. What we didn't know couldn't hurt us.

When the door closed behind them, I sat at the other side of the room, eating hot sandwiches and drinking, keeping my eye on the door, and waiting.

Everyone around was cheerful over my return and trying not to acknowledge what was happening in the back room. None of us, in all our hundreds of years, had ever talked about it.

I listened to the strained revelry around me, but kept my eyes on the door as I ate and drank, waiting, wondering what he was doing as the seconds passed.

And then I heard, from across the room and through the din of conversation and laughing, a small fist pounding on the door, accompanied by a small screaming voice. Then the door was thrown open and Sean did what no one else ever had; he made his escape.

He ran screaming and crying into the crowd, looking for the door and trying to get away.

Fat Man came out after him, stumbling, stomping and probably completely flabbergasted by the whole thing. This was not supposed to happen, had never happened before. His shirt was off and, if possible, he looked even fatter with his bulk now hanging free over the waistband of his pants. Still, he moved like a hurricane, big fat bastard or not. Sean only saved himself by ducking under a table and turning just in time to avoid Fat Man grabbing him by the neck.

He moved through the crowd with the determination of the condemned, and really, isn't that what he was. I mean, even if he got outside, where was he going to go?

He stepped between two guys I work with, and Fat Man had to shove them away to get past. Both of them flew across the room with the force of his push. Sean spotted one of the machines and climbed on top of it, then scurried higher, up onto one of the air vents, near the ceiling and completely out of reach of anyone in the plant.

From that height, he had a view of everyone. He found me, sitting on a stool and finishing off another sandwich.

"You said I was good," he yelled down to me. "You said I was gonna come and visit and then go back home."

Fat Man looked at me. I had to shrug, what else could I do? Tell him the truth, that I'd grabbed the wrong one?

"Hey," I said, "I had to tell the kid something to get him to come along, didn't I? Just get him down and eat him so we can get started on next year."

Fat Man was obviously very unhappy about the whole thing. He turned back toward the boy on the air vent and steam was practically coming off him. He grabbed the base of the air vent and just tore it off the machine. It came lose from the ceiling, almost collapsed, and Sean lost his grip. He fell and Fat Man caught him.

The boy kept struggling to get away, swinging his arms and trying to hit Santa, so Fat Man broke them. They snapped like twigs, and Sean's fighting stopped, replaced by agonized wailing.

He stomped past the onlookers, my friends, family, and coworkers all waiting for whatever was going to happen next, and carried the screaming child into the back room, slamming the door behind him. It sounded like Finality.

Everyone was quiet. We waited. We held our breath.

Suddenly from inside the room the boy screamed louder than he had so far, this high, ear-piercing, head-splitting scream that made all of us want to rip our own ears off just so we wouldn't hear that anymore.

And then, just as quickly as the screaming started, it was over. The following silence was thick with tension. The only thing to be heard in the entire shop was the hundreds of us finally letting out our breath. Things seemed, for a minute, to have returned to normal. This was all just a minor show, a distraction from the routine, but now it was over and we'd all go back to work and next year it would be the same thing all over again, except without the fanfare.

My supervisor appointed two guys to fix the air vent and they scurried off to get their tools.

I waited, though. I knew it *couldn't* have ended like that. There had to be more. I couldn't accept that that was it.

It wasn't.

The door flew open again and Fat Man came stumbling out. There was blood on his face and meat hanging from his mouth. One side of his face looked like it was melting. The whole left side of his body, he was dragging behind him. His eyes were fixed on me. I suddenly felt the room get a lot smaller and Fat Man was a little too close to me for comfort. I got off my stool and backed up a bit. He was coming right for me.

"What did you do?" he asked. "You grabbed the wrong one, didn't you?"

I shook my head, stammered, "I just—I just grabbed the one I saw. He was the one I was seeing, the one on the list."

"You grabbed the wrong one!" he yelled. His skin was boiling and chunks of it fell off, steaming when they hit the ground.

"No, honest," I said. "I just didn't see, I mean—."

"You mean you thought you'd pull a little trick on the boss, didn't you? Grab the good one instead of the bad one, huh? Pull a switch and see what happens?"

"No, I didn't. I promise, I—."

"Sure you did. Well." He stopped "This is what happens. Do you like it? Was this what you expected?"

One of his eyes fell out. It smacked the floor between us with a squish.

"Does this make you happy?"

I felt a lump the size of a softball go down my throat when I swallowed. Why was he still up? Why didn't he just go down and stay there?

All of us knew what could happen if he ate one of the good kids. He'd die. It was feeding off the bad ones that kept him going so long, we knew that, so why the hell hadn't he gone down yet? This was messed up, it had somehow not happened the way it was supposed to and now what was I going to do?

I did the only thing I could; I followed Sean's example and ran. He reached out and I felt his fingers graze the back of my neck, but he was weakened and I got away. I hit the door and got out into the snow. Fat Man was right behind me.

"You can't get away," he called. I was afraid he might be right.

As I ran, I had to wonder why no one else had stepped in. With so many of us, and Fat Man falling apart, literally, surely we could all take him down. So why was I running alone? Why were they all standing around watching? We'd all wanted him dead. It wasn't even something we had to discuss amongst ourselves; it was just a known fact. Fat Man had to go. And here I'd taken a big step toward that goal, but no one had jumped in to help.

He caught my ankle, but I twisted my foot, wrapped it around his wrist, and his hand snapped off. I kicked off the clutching fingers and gained some ground.

I looked over my shoulder to see where he was. He hadn't moved and was still looking at his broken hand lying in the snow. He looked up at me then and I saw most of the skin was gone from his face. The snow beneath him was growing more and more pink. Steam rose off him.

I thought I was home free. He'd never make it to me in time. It worked!

I turned around to keep the distance between us, and I ran into three of my coworkers.

"It's almost over," I told them.

"Yep," one of them said, then the other two grabbed my arms.

• • • •

I DON'T KNOW WHY THEY saved him. Maybe it's like I said earlier, without him we never would have made it as long as we have. But that's in the world with other people. We could make it up here by ourselves, I know we could. But they don't see it that way. We all hate Fat Man's ruthlessness, I know that without a doubt. None of the others want to be on the receiving end of his anger. But for some reason, still, they saved him. I'm not a child, nor am I a human, but I was very bad, and that goes a long way. He refused to eat me because then he couldn't punish me. So they fed him my arms, and my legs, and my eyes. They cut off my ears and he ate those, too. Then they sewed up the holes. I can still hear, they didn't take away the inner workings. But everything is muffled and I rely now on the vibrations I get from the sounds things make.

He ate what they fed him and slowly he recovered. I can't see, so I don't know if he returned to what he was before, but when my arms and legs had gone down, I saw some of his skin already growing back.

Now I sit in a corner of his office. He's got all the toys in the world, and I'm just the latest addition. He broke all of my teeth, then pulled what was left and now, when one of the others has been good, he lets them use me. I can't fight back, and he usually joins them, Fat Man at one end and the elf he's rewarding at the other. I close it all off. I replay the night in my head, wondering why none of them helped me. And I hope every year that someone else will get the same idea, and that this time the others will join in. Not that it would do me any good, but at least I'd know I wasn't going through all this for nothing. 'Till then, I'm here in my corner, in the dark and the cold, waiting for the next time they pull me out and split me in two—he's not just fat around the middle—thinking my thoughts, and still working for the Fat Man.

Prompt #9:

Write a story about your favorite holiday.

Or maybe not your favorite holiday, but any holiday.

Other holiday stories I've written are, obviously, "Working for the Fat Man" as well as:

1. New Year's Day
2. Martin Luther King Jr. Day
3. Groundhog Day
4. Ash Wednesday
5. Valentine's Day
6. Presidents' Day

TERRIBLE THRILLS

(for Christopher Fulbright and Eric Brown)
(originally published in Cyber-Pulp Halloween Anthology 2.0*)*

• • • •

Track One: The Murder

"TERRIBLE THRILLS," the CD cover announced. "Horrible Halloween Sound Effects Sure to Thrill You, Chill You, and Keep You Up All Night." There were two tracks.

Chris put the CD in his player and pushed PLAY, put the player in his window, and waited for the trick-or-treaters to show up.

The CD started quiet, and if Chris hadn't been listening, he wouldn't have been sure anything was coming out at all. But he heard it, just there, in the back. Breathing. Further away, metal clinked against metal.

Whoever was breathing let go a hitch, like they were trying to control their crying, and then Chris heard it. She wasn't breathing, she was whining, very high and in the back of her throat. Her voice was nearly gone from crying and screaming. And being strapped to a pole with her arms above her head so she could hardly catch a decent breath didn't help.

The doorbell rang and Chris leapt up, grabbed the candy bowl, and opened the door.

A small group of early starters stood huddled on his porch, bags at the ready, chanting the way children have, never really falling in all together, "Trick or treat." Chris made a comment about their scary costumes, then tossed a candy bar into each bag. They all said, "Thank you," and Chris closed the door as they were turning to step off the porch.

He sat back down and listened again to the CD.

The man wheeling the tray sneered and uttered something Chris couldn't make out, but the evil grin on the man's face was unmistakable. Chris felt his heart thud in his chest, wondering what the man was going to do to with the instrument he picked up. It was like a—.

The doorbell rang again and Chris hopped up and dragged his attention to the kids on his porch. After doling out the treats, he returned to his chair.

The man was pressing his blade into the woman's skin, slowly, and just the tip. The woman was grunting in the back of her throat, desperate not to scream, not to give him the satisfaction. But that blade was moving; not really pressing into her skin, rather moving slowly through it. And the ease with which he was doing it made it hurt worse. Of all the things he'd done to her tonight, this probably hurt more than all of them.

The doorbell rang again.

When he returned, Chris turned the CD player away from the window, turned it down a little, and moved up next to the speaker.

The man removed the blade and the woman let out her breath in a huge rush. He giggled. Her head lolled sideways, and her eyes moved up to his face and she asked, "Why?"

Chris sat up.

Had he been seeing this, or only hearing it? And if he was only hearing it, how was he filing in the rest of the details. He tried to think and remember what he'd actually *heard*, and what his mind had added.

Naturally, he'd only heard the woman's breathing, the instruments, then the woman making some noise in her effort not to scream. But where did the rest come from? He realized he'd even been about to name the man.

On the CD, the woman said, "Please, Edward. Please stop."

Edward. That's exactly what Chris was about to name him. Had she already said it earlier and Chris let it slip through his mind? He had been getting up every few minutes for the trick-or-treaters. She must have mentioned it before and he forgot.

The doorbell rang and Chris ignored it. He got up and shut off the porch light. The doorbell rang again, but he was already sitting with his ear to the speaker. After a few seconds, the footsteps went down his porch steps and vanished up the sidewalk to the next house.

Chris listened.

Edward looked at the girl and grinned—but how did Chris know this?—then reached up and grabbed her by the throat. He squeezed. Her eyes bulged and she tried to cough, but Edward's grip was too tight. Spit gathered on her lips. Her eyes bulged. Her face was red. With his free hand, Edward sliced off one of her nipples. She didn't have enough strength or breath to scream.

Alice—that was her name, Chris was sure of it—made some gurgling sound, trying to cough, trying to force air through her throat despite Edward's iron hands. Then he let go and she collapsed, pulling the restraints taut, hanging halfway down the pole he'd strapped her to. Alice glanced up. There was T-bar at the top of the pole. That's what Edward had strapped her to and if she could just . . . no, she saw that even getting the straps off the bar, she'd still be wrapped around the pole. She wasn't going to get out of here, not until Edward was finished with her, and she knew she'd be dead by then. The pain in her nipple drowned out most of the other pain in her body now.

She struggled to get her feet under her again. At least then she'd be able to breathe.

Edward slapped her. Her eyes opened and she lifted her head, more aware now. Edward held up a curling iron. The red light in the handle was glowing.

"Shh," Edward said. He put the hot metal against her nipple.

She leapt backward, struggling in her restraints like an animal in a trap, trying to move, to get away, to just stay alive long enough for him to stop. But Edward grabbed her body and held her tight so her struggles were small and insignificant.

He let her go again, vanished, and when he came back into view, he was rolling a television up close to her.

"Watch this," he said. He turned on the screen and Alice was horrified to see herself. The quality was bad, the light was barely there, but it was enough to know what was happening. She couldn't see him, but she knew she was watching herself on top of Tony. She knew that because Tony liked her on top. Edward preferred her in the submissive and he never let her get on top. But Tony loved it, and Edward had somehow got it on tape.

At least now she understood why he was doing this. But how far would it go? Would he really kill her? She'd thought it just a second ago, but would he really? He would almost have to, wouldn't he? He couldn't do all the things he'd done to her tonight and just let her go.

"This is my favorite part," Edward said. She watched herself in the middle of an orgasm, whining and writhing on Tony. "You really like what he's got, don't you?" Edward asked.

Alice watched the screen. Edward stepped in front of her, punched her in the face and yelled, "I said you really like what he's got, don't you?"

She nodded her head. No point in lying, was there?

"Well, if you like it so much, you might as well have it," he said. She didn't see where he pulled it from, but something hit her in the face. He held it up for her to see. It hung limp in his fingers, shriveled and hairy.

All doubts she had about how far Edward would go were wiped away. She knew now he wouldn't stop until he simply couldn't go any further. But how far would that be?

"Here, watch this part," Edward said.

She looked up again. Tony was on his back. She bent over him, her head bobbing up and down.

"You look like you're enjoying that, too," Edward said. "Let's see how much you really like what he's got."

He wrenched open her jaw and shoved the whole thing in her mouth. He snapped her mouth shut, slapped a length of duct tape over it, and stood back.

Chris lurched backward, his leg flew up, and he knocked his CD player onto the floor. The door fell open and the CD rolled across the floor. He sat up.

"What?" he said. The phone was ringing.

He struggled up to get it, but the machine was quicker.

"Hey man," Eric's voice came through the speaker. "Just got home, thought I'd see what's going on. Call me later."

Chris looked around. It was dark outside now. Trick-or-treaters walked up and down the sidewalks, all of them passing his house without stopping. He remembered he'd shut out the porch light. He turned it back on now.

He turned on the light and located the CD, then put it into its jewel case and set it aside. He must have dozed off or something. With that thing playing in the background, he'd had one hell of a dream. And it had seemed so real.

His chest itched, but when he scratched it, he flinched when his fingers brushed his nipple. He pulled his shirt collar down and saw somehow he'd gotten a burn on his nipple.

"Hmm," he said. "Wonder when I did that." But before he could think about it any longer, the doorbell rang. He opened it to an uneven chorus of kids chanting "Trick or treat!"

· · · ·

<u>Track Two: The Mayhem</u>

ERIC HUNG UP THE PHONE and picked up the CD. *Terrible Thrills, huh?* he thought. *We'll see.*

He put the CD in his stereo, hit PLAY, and looked at the back cover while the first track started. There was silence, and then, very quiet, breathing and metal instruments.

"What's this crap?" he asked. "The Murder? Sure thing." *Heard that cheap ass stuff before. More bad actresses and their pathetic screaming.* He hit the forward track button and was met by a ringing chorus of bells and whistles, sirens and screams. "That's mayhem, all right," Eric said.

He let the track play while he opened the bags of candy and dumped them into a big plastic bowl. Before he could even set it down, the doorbell rang.

"Trick or treat," the two kids on the porch cried. One was dressed as a clown. The other some cartoon character Eric had seen but wasn't familiar with.

"Nice costumes," he said, lowering the bowl so the kids could grab what they wanted.

Behind him, the sounds got louder and more frenzied. There was a bass beat underneath the chaos. He glanced up at the kids' father who was standing just off to the side of the porch. The father caught his eye, smiled like people do when they don't know what else to do . . . then his expression changed.

The brow furrowed and the eyes got dark. The father's chest puffed out and he stepped up onto the porch, shoved his way between the two kids, and stepped into Eric's living room.

Eric stepped back and asked, "What are you doing?" but that was as far as he got. The man raised a fist and punched Eric in the nose. Eric fell down and tried to catch the blood gushing down his face.

"What the fuck?" he asked. The man ignored him and stepped up between Eric's legs, brought his arms up. Eric rolled out of the way before the man brought his elbow into the floor.

He got to his feet and rushed at the crazy man like a football player, carrying him back through the door and shoving him off the porch. Eric ran inside, slammed and locked the door, and looked out the window to see what was happening.

There was a siren and a scream and he thought *Did someone call the police?* Then he realized the sounds were coming from his stereo. He turned around and was going to shut it off, but before he hit the button, there came a BANG and a rattle. He turned toward the sound. The crazy man was pounding on the window. *He'll break it soon*, Eric thought.

Another sound from the other window and Eric turned to see the man's kids staring at him, their palms against the glass, fingers splayed. Their eyes were blank.

"What's going on here?" he asked, but they didn't hear. He doubted they would have answered anyway.

He watched Dad disappear from view, come back a second later with a fallen branch. Dad swung it, shattered the glass, and climbed into the house. Eric noticed a dribble of blood from the man's ear just before he turned and dashed into the kitchen.

He grabbed a knife from the block, then went for the phone. Dad beat him to it, swung the log again and shattered the plastic.

"Get out of here!" Eric yelled over the crashes and squeals coming from his stereo.

Dad grinned and showed bloody teeth. The blood from his ear had ran down to his neck and was soaking into the collar of his shirt.

"What's your problem, man?"

The children were trying to climb in through the broken window, but they were too short. Dad stood still for a second, he and Eric waiting for the other to make their move.

This is like that Romero movie, Eric thought. He slashed out with the knife, but was too far away, and not really committed to the act and his swing came up far too short. Dad, however, was fully invested and when he swung the log, it knocked Eric into the wall. Eric dropped the knife, tried to grab it, missed, and decided to just get away.

He ran for the front door; he'd call the police from the neighbor's.

He opened it and stepped out, tripped over one of the children. Eric hit his face on the porch. The Clown grabbed his leg and bit into it. Eric screamed. The Cartoon Kid stood over him and started beating him with a smaller log than his father held, but still big enough to hurt.

Eric put his arms up for protection and didn't see Dad stumbling outside. But he felt the blow when the man brought the log down hard into Eric's groin. He wanted to pass out, but survival is a tough instinct to beat. He managed to twist himself so the blows connected with his back. He pushed himself up, shook the Clown off his leg, suffering horrible pain when the kid tore away a piece of Eric with him, and was able to shove Dad aside. Dad tripped over The Cartoon Kid and fell backward.

From inside glass shattered, dogs barked, horns blared. The mayhem played on.

Eric went in, closed and locked the door again, then went to the broken window.

There were more people on the street and Eric yelled at one, "Hey! You! Call the police, man, this dude's trying to kill me!"

The trick-or-treater, a pre-teen dressed as a hobo, came closer and asked, "What?"

Another siren went off, followed by an electric sizzle.

The Hobo stopped in his tracks, got the strangest look on his face, and suddenly ran and charged Eric's front door. He hit it straight on with his head, bust it open, and fell forward.

Eric couldn't believe any of this. What the hell was happening to people?

Through the open window, Dad grabbed Eric's shirt and hauled him backward through the pane. Glass snagged Eric's shirt, ripped it, tore into his back. He screamed.

Dad pulled him out to the middle of the front yard.

Eric's next door neighbor, an old man who'd always seemed like a pleasant guy if Eric had gotten to know him, came out onto his porch and shouted, "What the hell is all this—," and then he stopped. He stared into space for a second and, in the pause, Eric heard bells ringing. Then the old man looked down at Eric, stepped off his porch, and came around his fence to Eric's yard. Dad had stopped moving and seemed to be waiting. Eric, too. The old man came up next to Eric, then kicked him in the head.

Eric struggled to get up, but the more people who came to help him, the more people it seemed were suddenly trying to kill him. And the wounds from the glass didn't help. He tried again to get up, but The Hobo stepped on his chest. The Clown found his place again and gnawed on Eric's leg.

He heard whistles and sirens.

Dad leaned down and bit into Eric's side. The Cartoon Kid picked up Eric's arm. The Hobo put his mouth over Eric's face and tried to tear it off. With his sight gone, Eric didn't see the old man pick up the rock. He wanted to open the skull and get to the brain.

The bells rang, sirens wailed, horns sounded, dogs barked, wind blew, demons screamed, angels cried, the dead pleaded mercy, and every trick-or-treater who tried to come to Eric's rescue was soon swayed by the chorus and joined in the feast.

The stereo played on into the morning.

Take a **common trope and reverse it.** For example, in the following story, I wrote about a vampire who doesn't stalk his prey, but is instead drawn to them. Then I had to figure out HOW is he drawn to them? At the time I was listening to Prince's then-new RAINBOW CHILDREN album, and the song "Family Name" provided the answer.

Other stories using this prompt include:

1. Blue Moon Story (werewolf who only changes during a blue moon)
2. Pest Control (a zombie story replacing zombies with bugs)
3. When Jessica Went Home (vampire story in which the unborn baby is a vampire but the pregnant mother isn't, and she must still manage to feed him)
4. Timesmiths (time travel story from the perspective of someone who is living through the constantly shifting time stream)
5. Reckoning (a ghost story in which a man is haunted by himself)

FAMILY NAME

· · · ·

JODY LURCHED DOWN THE wet street, the air chilly from the recent rain and the streetlights reflecting off the water, clutching his stomach and trying to breathe. His face was pale and he was sweating. His vision had blurred to the point he could make out nothing but bright red line the glowed ahead of him, leading him on, and Jody followed it like a servant. The red line turned off the sidewalk, up a concrete stoop, and into an apartment building. Jody turned and followed it up and in, up a flight of stairs, up another, around a corner, down a hall. The red line stopped in front of a door. Jody stared at it. His vision swam. He knocked on the door, trying not to pound. The ache in his stomach twisted, churning heat roiling inside. A sound came from inside, the high yapping of a small dog he thought. He knocked again. A voice cursed, then asked who is it? Jody hit the door with the little force he could muster and it appeared to be enough; the door flew inward from the busted lock. Jody's hands grabbed the small dog, threw it against the wall, then reached for the tired man standing there, pulled him close, and he sank his teeth into the man's neck. The pain went away and his vision cleared. The red line was gone.

· · · ·

JODY LEFT THE BODY, no longer concerned with concealing his crimes. In fact, he'd begun to hope people would see what he'd done, make the leap of faith concerning their nature, and come after him, stakes at the ready. But so far, he'd gone unpunished. And his desire to be stopped aside, he still hid in the sewers and the dark places. After the rain, the sewers would be too wet, so he'd have to find something else for now, and quickly from the looks of the sky. He considered an abandoned building he saw up the street, but that wouldn't do.

Chances were too good it was already occupied by squatters. In the end, he spent the day buried deep in a fast food trash dumpster beneath broken down cardboard boxes and heavy sacks of old food and leaking drink cups. The rats kept him company.

He was glad he didn't mind the rats because they feasted near his feet. God knew how they got up inside the dumpster, but they'd managed somehow. He fell asleep listening to their squeaks. His stomach was full and his dreams were disturbing.

• • • •

THE METABOLISM OF A vampire was slower than a normal man's, Jody had learned. He didn't need to drink every night, and for that he was glad. On the nights he was free of the thirst, he went into the streets and the lights, wanting to feel normal again among the people. The first night, he'd met a woman and gone home with her. After suffering an impotent humiliation, he swore that wouldn't happen again, so now he only went for the company of many. And when someone wanted to get closer, he kindly declined. Tonight, however, still stinking of garbage, Jody didn't think that would be a concern. In fact, he didn't think it would be long before he'd have to find some other way to be around people. The longer his condition continued, the worse he smelled. Without putting the thought into words, he didn't think he could bring himself to do that, he knew it was the smell of earth and death.

He walked straight and steady, relishing this break from the tremors of his thirst.

He'd lost himself in a million thoughts and it wasn't until he stopped and looked around that he realized he'd walked all the way to The Strip, the part of town it was usually best to stay away from at night. He was about turn the corner and make his way back to somewhere brighter and friendlier when a light flashed, a siren beeped, and he heard the crunch of tires over gravel.

A flashlight shone on him.

He was being stopped for vagrancy, he imagined. Under normal circumstances, he figured they'd direct him to a shelter, or, if he turned out to be tanked, maybe they'd take him in for the night and let him go in the morning. Isn't that what they did in movies, put the drunks in the drunk tank to let them sleep it off. He'd kindly thank them, then head off toward whatever shelter they named and when they were gone, so would he be.

He turned around and for a brief second couldn't remember what he'd just been thinking.

Jody and Officer Kirby Cook had been cousins before Jody . . . before this happened to him. And now both stared at each other, slack-jawed and wide-eyed, neither believing what they were seeing.

The night had gone chilly. Jody shivered, put his arms around himself.

"Jody?" Kirby asked, leaning across the seat and calling out the window. "Jody?"

Jody said nothing, only turned around and walked on, if he was quick enough he could be around the corner and gone into the shadows. He couldn't turn into a bat or a mist or anything, but he was pretty quick now and he was sure he could get up the nearest fire escape before Kirby had time to park his cruiser and get out to follow.

Instead of getting out, however, Kirby rolled after him, shouting Jody's name out the window and keeping that damned light on him.

When Jody didn't stop, Kirby flashed the lights again, turned on the siren, this time the loud, long whining, not the short burst he'd let go earlier. Jody got around the corner, but Kirby was right behind him and Jody finally stopped, put his hands up, and turned around.

Kirby kept Jody pinned down in the light, parked his car and got out, walking slowly toward his cousin, unbelief on his face.

"Jody?" he asked for the third time. "What . . ."

"Just turn around, Kirby," Jody said. "Please, just leave it alone and forget it."

"I don't think so. Get in the car, we gotta talk apparently."

"There's nothing to say. Look at me."

"What happened?"

"I don't know. Let it go. Turn around and forget it like I said. Believe me, this isn't something you can help me with."

How did he get here, Jody wondered. Ten minutes ago he was wandering the streets in search of people and lights, and now he was trying to get away from one of the people he should be glad to see.

"How did you get here?" Kirby asked.

Jody didn't answer, but he let loose a quick, sharp laugh that cut the tone of the last few minutes, but did nothing to lighten the tension.

"What's so funny?"

"I'm leaving now," Jody said, and before Kirby could to stop him, Jody leapt to the fire escape, scurried up, and vanished over the roof and into the dark.

●●●●

NOTHING CAME TOO CLEAR to his mind lately. He didn't know how long he'd been in this state, the days all ran together. He'd seen the bright red line at least three times, but it might have been more. He knew his name and he knew where his house was, but the one time he'd returned he found it closed and yellow tape covered the front door. When that first sunrise came and his head began to pound, it didn't take long to put together the night's events and figure out what he was, there were only so many possibilities when Jody had dug himself out of the ground, found his house was a crime scene, and the daylight made him sick. He didn't know how his father played into this; Dad had been dead a year, but Jody knew he was a part of it somehow. And then there was that red line. When he saw it the first time, he didn't understand, but he followed it anyway. And the more he followed it, the more everything else went milky until the only thing he knew for certain was the direction of that red line, like a painted neon marker to lead him. Where had it gone? He couldn't remember, but he knew he felt better afterward.

He was so lonely anymore, he wanted to feel better around people. He wanted that sense of the familiar to put him at ease, but so far it had only been a haze of faces and an echo of voices swimming in his head. None of it had connected with him, and nothing had made him feel normal. Whatever reality he'd known before, he was realizing slowly over the course of the pounding nights he suffered that he would never get any of it back. Now there was only this emptiness inside, and that red line.

But still he kept trying.

There was a bar on Ninth Street he used to like because it had good music in the juke box and live bands on Fridays. He didn't know what day it was, but if nothing else he could sit in the corner, stay in the dark, and listen to juke.

It never occurred to him he'd be seen by someone who knew him. And whether it was coincidence or the workings of a simple universe, all Jody knew was the a while after he sat down, someone called his name and when Jody looked up, there stood Kirby again.

Jody's head began to pound.

His cousin was in Jody's booth before Jody could react, sliding in too quickly to let Jody escape, trapping him against the wall.

"I hoped I might see you again," Kirby said. He wasn't in uniform tonight. "You're not as easy to track down as I'd thought."

Jody sat against the wall and watched the seat across from him, saying nothing.

"Where've you been?" Kirby asked. "It's been over a week since I saw you on the street, and now you show up here, Jody, what the hell is going on?"

A week? Where had the time gone? It seemed like he'd only seen Kirby last night, maybe the night before. A week, though?

"I helped carry you to the hearse," Kirby said. "What's going on?"

Jody ignored him and hoped the pounding behind his eyes stopped soon or else his head would explode and then Kirby'd have no one to question.

A second later, Jody was hauled out of the booth and was being dragged to the door. The bartender tried to stop Kirby, but the cop showed his badge and the bartender backed up. Jody was shoved into the back of Kirby's car. This wasn't his cruiser, but Kirby's own beat up Reliant. Jody wanted to get out and run away again, but the pain in his temples was incredible and all he could do was put his head in his hands and wish for the night to be over.

Before he knew it, the car stopped and Kirby was pulling him from the back seat.

"You're going to talk to me," his cousin said, hauling Jody in his house, closing and locking the door, and bringing him to the couch. "I'm not going to pretend to understand this, Jody, but if you're here, something's going on because I was at your funeral, I know the cop who found you, so I want you to answer one question for me."

He pointed to something in front of Jody.

"Did you do this?"

Jody followed the angle of Kirby's finger, a hard enough task with his eyes burning like they did, and saw there was a coffee table in front of him, covered with big black and white sheets. He looked closer and saw they were photos. He was trying to make sense of them in his mind, but before he could focus too closely, everything vanished again and the red line glowed under him. He saw it, watched it, followed it, across the floor, knowing that wherever it went, there Jody would find comfort. It stopped in front shortly. Jody didn't see what stood at the other end, someone or something, he didn't care. He leapt and fell upon whatever it was, and something screamed with a familiar voice.

Jody filled himself with blood, each swallow drowning out that awful pain in his head. It dwindled inch by inch until the space behind his eyes was a calm lake, and he finally lifted his head and sighed, satisfied.

· · · ·

HE'D DONE IT AGAIN.

And this time it had been so sudden. Always before there'd been warning as the ache swelled and finally the line grew ahead of him. But this time it had just stopped, and while he couldn't understand why, he knew he felt three hundred percent better. The only ache now was the loneliness and the loss of his past. But sometimes, when the pain in his head was finally gone, he thought he could live with the rest.

He stood up and stretched, heavy again and full, knowing it would be daylight too soon for him to get anywhere safe. He looked around and saw he was still inside. In that case, he'd clean up whatever mess there was, then hide beneath a pile of clothes in someone's closet until nightfall.

He shook the stiffness from his limbs, the sleep from his head, and bent to grab the body. When he did, his eyes fell upon the coffee table and he vaguely recalled someone trying to show him something once on a table like this. Black and white sheets, like photos. Jody picked one up and stared at it.

The blood in his stomach began to rise into his throat when he saw, very clearly, a picture of his aunt Dorothy with wide, empty eyes, and blood covering her from the neck down. Jody dropped this shot and grabbed another. Here was his brother, Tony. Dead, also, his throat torn out. Another photo showed another relative, one who's name he didn't recall, a second or third cousin he'd met at a family reunion once, again with dead eyes and blood pooling under the body.

What is this, he wondered. What's happening? Did I . . . ?

He picked up another picture and recognized his uncle Jack. Paper clipped to this was a picture of Jack's dog, limp against a wall with blood coming from its mouth. He'd always hated that dog, he remembered.

As if the loneliness weren't enough, he thought, the entire family is gone. Almost. He scanned the pictures, trying to figure out who was left. He didn't see his mother, and that was good. But a voice in the back of his head told him that he would be seeing her eventually, wouldn't he? Yes, he figured he would after all, because he never knew where that red line was going to take him, but he did know one thing with absolute certainty: when it appeared, there was nothing Jody could do but follow it.

He hauled Kirby's body into the bedroom, closed the door, drew the blinds. He stepped into the closet, buried himself under shirts, coats, and a couple of blankets from the top shelf. When he woke up, he decided, he would try to make it as far north as he could. He had family up there, relatives he didn't know and wouldn't miss. He knew the red line would be back. The least he could do was try to get there before it did and spare the ones he loved most.

. . . .

THANK YOU FOR READING this book. I hope you will consider leaving an honest review.

• • • •

IF YOU WOULD LIKE TO keep up to date on my writing and where it can be found, why not join my FREE weekly newsletter HERE[1].

---

1. https://cdennismoore.us3.list-manage.com/

subscribe?u=98166cbe6a6ccf1d7a39e772e&id=ac9e73819c

Don't miss out!

Visit the website below and you can sign up to receive emails whenever C. Dennis Moore publishes a new book. There's no charge and no obligation.

https://books2read.com/r/B-A-EPXB-LEYK

Connecting independent readers to independent writers.

Did you love *10 Writing Prompts That Work (and the stories to prove it)*? Then you should read *Doing it Write*[2] by C. Dennis Moore!

Whether you're a new writer or a veteran, many of the pitfalls are the same. Lack of motivation, writer's block, outside influences, and lack of belief in yourself can all contribute to relying on the dreaded day job. But if you're looking for a way to break the cycle and be the consistently productive writer you've always known you could be, DOING IT WRITE will help.

This guide starts off with the basics: how to set up your writing space, where to write, desk placement, and even desk organization. Then it moves on to real talk.

Everything is covered here, from making the choice to be a writer, to time management to how believing in yourself can lead to others

---

2. https://books2read.com/u/31MolD

3. https://books2read.com/u/31MolD

believing in you too. This book helps you not only set and prioritize goals, but also provides a realistic system for achieving them.

DOING IT WRITE teaches you how to change your mindset and stop being your own worst enemy when it comes to your work. It shows you how to deal with perceptions, your own personal values and rules, as well as your identity as a writer.

And what's more important, DOING IT WRITE will help you to learn how to maintain healthy relationships with all the non-writers in your life. It will also show you how to live healthier while not having to give up time in the seat every day. This book challenges the notion of writing being a marathon and teaches you how to reward yourself for a job well done. Finally, DOING IT WRITE teaches you how to raise and maintain your own standards and be the hero of your own story.

There are many writing how-to books out there, but DOING IT WRITE is not one of them. DOING IT WRITE is the result of nearly 30 years of experience in the writing field. It's a how-to-LIVE book, written for writers.

About the Author

C. Dennis Moore is the author of the Angel Hill novels, the Monsters of Green Lake series, as well as the Holiday Horrors. He lives in St. Joseph, MO with his wife, Kara. They have seven children and three grandchildren.